Every so often the world of sport throws up an event or performance quite out of the ordinary. Cricket has enjoyed more than its fair share of such moments. The events of 1981, however, captured the public's imagination in an unprecedented way. It provided not one match but three packed with extraordinary incidents and Test cricket enjoyed its highest popularity for years.

In the Third Test, England recovered from the brink of defeat to overcome odds of 500-1 and win by 18 runs. A fortnight later they bowled out Australia for 121 in their fourth innings to win the game by 29 runs. In the Fifth Test, the margin was greater but the change of fortune just as dramatic. The Sixth Test included three centuries, Dennis Lillee's best bowling Test performance ever, and a nail-biting finish. It ended in a draw. Overshadowing all of this was the performance of one man – Ian Botham, who had failed in the first two Tests and resigned the captaincy. In the next three Tests he scored two of the finest innings ever seen and produced a match-winning bowling performance of 5 wickets for 11 runs. And of course there was Mike Brearley's contribution as captain. He demonstrated that captaincy really *can* win matches. In addition, his leadership brought out the best in his players in an extraordinary cricket season.

By the same author (with Dudley Doust)

THE RETURN OF THE ASHES
THE ASHES RETAINED

Phoenix from the Ashes

Phoenix from the
Ashes

The story of the England-Australia Series 1981

Mike Brearley

Foreword by IAN BOTHAM

London
UNWIN PAPERBACKS
Boston   Sydney

First published in Great Britain by Hodder and Stoughton Limited 1982
First published by Unwin Paperbacks 1983
This book is copyright under the Berne Convention. No reproduction
without permission. All rights reserved.

UNWIN® PAPERBACKS
40 Museum Street, London, WC1A 1LU, UK

Unwin Paperbacks,
Park Lane, Hemel Hempstead, Herts HP2 4TE, UK

George Allen & Unwin Australia Pty Ltd,
8 Napier Street, North Sydney, NSW 2060, Australia

© Mike Brearley Ltd 1982

British Library Cataloguing in Publication Data

Brearley, Mike
    Phoenix from the Ashes.
    1. Cricket – England   2. Cricket – Australia
    I. Title
    796.35'865   GV928.G7
    ISBN 0–04–796072–8

Set in 10 on 11 point Palatino by Nene Phototypesetters, Northampton
and printed in Great Britain by Cox and Wyman Ltd, Reading

Contents

		page	
	Acknowledgments	*page*	vi
	Foreword by Ian Botham		ix
	Preface		xi
1	The Hollow Crown		1
2	Australia Go One Up		9
3	Ready for the Call		31
4	No More Skylarks		48
5	The Headingley Test		65
6	Lightning Strikes Twice		91
7	Interlude		118
8	A Great Century		129
9	Lillee's Last Laugh		155
10	Of Beer and Breweries		172
	Index		183

Acknowledgments

I should like to thank some of those who have helped me with this book. Jacki Warbrook, M. N. Patel and Len Wynne have efficiently and patiently typed out my almost illegible scripts. Jim Coldham has contributed the index, excellent as usual. Richard Cohen, the book's editor, has been particularly helpful, not to mention helpfully particular. He is totally responsible for any errors in what follows. I am also grateful to the *Sunday Times*, for which I wrote several articles during the summer about the Test series.

My previous books were written with Dudley Doust; in these collaborations his contribution was more substantial than that of the usual 'ghost', and from them I learned enough to risk branching out alone. Dudley continued to help with *Phoenix* by reading my early drafts and offering valuable criticism and encouragement. (He has also helped with Ian's foreword!)

Derek Randall, in his speech after receiving the man of the match award in the Centenary Test at Melbourne, thanked Dennis Lillee for 't' bump on my head', adding that if he had hit him anywhere else it might have hurt. I too should like to thank Dennis not only for regular bruises to body and ego, but for taking the trouble to write a postscript to this Pommie view of a series that in some respects he would prefer to forget.

Finally, Ian Botham and the rest of the England team, to whom I dedicate this book; in memory of a fantastic summer and a concerted effort. Their successes were, of course, my good fortune. Ian stood out like a colossus. He has been kind enough to contribute not only most of the runs, wickets and catches, but also a few words with which to kick off, so to speak.

List of illustrations

1. The author and Ian Botham.

2. Willis was unlucky in the first innings at Headingley. Hughes's reactions were pretty quick in self-preservation. He made 89.

3. A moment of realisation and delight. It *wasn't* a no-ball. Willis bowls Bright to win the Headingley Test.

4. Boycott hugs his 'amiable gorilla'. Botham was named man of the match at Edgbaston after his final spell of 5 wickets for 1 run.

5. A typical Lillee appeal. Boycott is the batsman. Lillee enjoyed his usual controversial exchanges with the umpires.

6. Botham crashes a ball through mid-off for four during his great second innings century at Old Trafford.

7. Botham bowling at the Oval. Despite injury he got through 89 overs and took ten wickets in the match.

8. The perfect fast bowler's action. Lillee is the finest bowler I have played against. In the final Oval Test he had his best Test performance (7 for 89) and took eleven wickets in the match.

9. Marsh is well placed but Gooch is yorked by Bright in the Fourth Test.

10. Marsh appeals against Boycott. Bright got one to turn sharply.

11. Marsh batting at the Oval. Knott sent champagne to Marsh at Headingley when the latter passed his world record for Test victims.

12.   Alderman listens to Lillee's advice. They finished with a combined total of 81 wickets in the six Tests. Alderman was the most successful of all bowlers in the series.

13.   Bright has given me too much room for Hughes's comfort at silly-point.

14.   Walking off at the Oval after my last Test innings.

Picture Credits

Illustrations by: Gerald Broadhead pages 34 and 179
Ranan Lurie page 135
The Times page 176

Photographs by: Sporting Pictures (UK) Ltd.: no. 1, Jack Hickes Ltd.: nos 2 and 3, Adrian Murrell/All Sport: nos. 4, 6, 7, 8 and 10, Ken Kelly: nos. 5, 9, 11 and 12, Patrick Eagar: nos 13 and 14

Foreword

Phoenix from the Ashes is a terrific job. It's an opportunity to read Brearley like a book. Which is fair enough: he's done it enough to us over the years.

I particularly like the stuff in Chapter 9 about telling me to cut out the short run and bowl properly. Bowl properly! Here was an old man, standing in the slips, complaining about his feet aching, and all the while telling me to bowl properly when I'd already bowled forty straight overs. I don't know what it is, but I took stuff from him that I'd clip other guys round the ear for.

There is something about Brears. He knows how I feel and what I'm thinking. He makes better communication with players than any other captain I've known. I'm often asked to compare him with Keith Fletcher. They both think a lot about the game on and off the field, and in that way they are similar. They both got a lot out of me. But they have different styles. Fletch doesn't say much; he just kicks you up the backside – which, by the time he got hold of me, was okay. I was a mature player. Brears went deeper and, I suppose, he had to, because I was younger and less experienced.

He was my first England captain and the role he played was very important. I'm not a particularly moody person and I very rarely get depressed, but sometimes, especially when I was under Brears, I would get stroppy. His reaction was not to get fussed. He just expected me to get on with it.

I'll always remember Mike at Headingley, the first time we'd met since he took over my job as captain. His behaviour struck me as odd. He was a bit too bubbly, either out of nerves or excitement, when he came up to the nets. 'D'you want to play?' he said to me, 'or do you want to be left out?'

Left out? Me? I thought he was crazy until, suddenly, I realised that he knew full well that I wanted to play. It wasn't a serious offer. It had been a gesture, acknowledging that I'd had a hard time and that being in the limelight might not be so easy for me.

That incident was probably the only awkward moment between me and Brears over the captaincy. He was always a replacement I could easily accept. Once he'd got his beard shaved off he was the same old Brears to me. For months I had been his understudy, his apprentice, and it seemed only natural that if I left the job I would hand it back to him. In hindsight, I feel I was his 'caretaker' captain.

At the end of this book, Brears pays me a nice compliment, comparing me to W. G. Grace. But he suggests I might not be that good if I'm allowed to take on the burden of the England captaincy again. I think he's wrong. It wasn't the captaincy that brought me down in 1981. I don't care what anybody says, no matter how good you are, you have a bad period in your career, and I genuinely believe that mine just happened to come at the time of my captaincy. It's a funny thing, but when I packed it in I felt I was just beginning to get the hang of the job, starting to be able to take it in my stride and not worrying about my own game.

I don't want it back soon. I've had a gutful of the job for four or five more years. But, nearer to the end of my career, I'd like to have it back: just to prove I can do it.

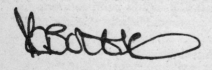

IAN BOTHAM

Preface

It is almost two years since the Headingley Test of 1981.
On the international front, three highly sponsored tours
of South Africa have rocked the boat of Test cricket without actually capsizing it. Before the first of them, England
lost the series in India 1–0 under Keith Fletcher, who was
promptly (prematurely, in my opinion) sacked. With Bob
Willis as captain (and without those who played for the
Breweries XI in South Africa, who had been banned from
Test cricket for three years), we beat India convincingly at
home. We won narrowly against an uneven Pakistan.
Their team had in Imran Khan and Abdul Qadir, both a
fast bowler of such brilliance and panache as to match
Dennis Lillee at his best, and a leg-spinner capable of
reviving an almost lost art.

Then to Australia in 1982/3, with many inexperienced
players, where England lost the Ashes to a better side.
The margin, however, was only 2–1, in a five-match
series: a much better performance, at least on paper, than
ours in 1979/80 when we lost all three Tests (but had
prudently declined to put the Ashes at stake). What is
more, in comparison with both the earlier series, Ian
Botham enjoyed only modest success. The hero of 1981
did not once take five wickets in an innings or make a
single score higher than 65. If he had performed at this
level in 1981, this book would not have been written.

But the events of the recent tour – with their
tremendous performances by Willis, Bob Taylor, Allan
Lamb and particularly by the impish Derek Randall and
the mature David Gower – will be forgotten when one
match is remembered: the Melbourne Test of December
1982. The result – a win for England by three runs – is the
narrowest in the whole history of Test cricket. If there
was an umbrella on the ground, it would have been lucky

to escape the fate of its predecessor at the Oval in 1902, whose handle was gnawed through by an ageing member.

Coming so soon after the remarkable finishes at Headingley and Edgbaston in 1981, the match at Melbourne reminds one that a climax that has built up slowly over several days and rounds off the individual little dramas of each delivery – there will have been at least 2,000 of them – creates a tension as gripping as in any sport. Even the video-taped highlights of those matches in England I still find nerve-wracking, as if time might be rolled back and the results reversed.

I hope that this reprint in paperback of *Phoenix from the Ashes* will enable new readers to recapture the excitement of those games. I also hope that these pages will give the reader an idea of what it's like to be involved in Test cricket, and some insight into the personality and achievement of the man whose performances might have come from *Boy's Own Paper* – Ian Botham.

1

The Hollow Crown

On 31 May 1980, as Middlesex were about to start a county match against Somerset at Taunton, I was called to the phone before play. Alec Bedser, chairman of the England selectors, told me that they had decided to 'give Ian a go' as captain for the Tests. Thus Ian Botham, aged 24, was thrown into the deepest of deep ends.

I was not surprised by the news. Three months before, at the end of the tour of Australia (when we lost 3–0), I had announced that I would not be available for future tours, mainly because I wanted to get on with my training in psychoanalysis, a process which had been delayed for some years by winter cricket. Moreover, I had that very week received a letter from Charlie Elliott, one of Alec's co-selectors, thanking me for all I had done as captain of England!

Anyway, Ian had already partially succeeded me, as he had just come from captaining England in the one-day Internationals at Headingley and Lord's. However, these matches were a mere preamble to the hardships ahead, specifically, five Tests against the West Indies (the most powerful side in the world), the Centenary Test against Australia, and then an expedition to the Caribbean for five more Tests against the West Indies. In spite of the evidence and of Ian's successes in the one-day matches, I still entertained a sneaking hope that I might be re-appointed for the first two or three Tests. I thought that this would have enabled me to help Ian, in the knowledge that he would take over from me later. It would also give him some cushion for the rigours of the chapel-seat of captaincy, and by putting off the start of the honeymoon period would also delay the onset of marital disillusions – at least until he was embarked on the winter tour. In many ways it is easier to captain England abroad. For one thing, you know you have the job for the duration of the tour; for another, the criticisms that hurt are always those of one's own crowds and media, and on tour such hostility is comfortably distant.

However, the news was neither unexpected nor entirely unwelcome to me. Though my timing might have been different, Botham would have been my choice too, so I had no difficulty in congratulating him warmly before the start of the game at Taunton. And in mid-afternoon, when he came in to bat, I happily greeted him in mid-pitch with a little gesture of *namaste* – the Indian greeting of respect. There were similarities between our encounter on this particular day and another coincidence of the fixture-list some seven years before, when Ray Illingworth, sacked the previous day as England captain, had to toss up at Folkestone with his successor, Mike Denness, at the start of Leicestershire's match with Kent. We, by contrast, felt no awkwardness or embarrassment – unless it was the underlying emotions that caused Ian to edge his second ball within my reach at first slip and me to fail to move let alone catch it! At close of play, I still felt animatedly involved in the post as the two of us discussed candidates for the Tests (our views were then very similar) and our chances against West Indies. It was only later in the evening, when I had left behind the buzz of cricket talk and the excitements of the day, that I allowed myself to feel the loss at this watershed in my life. There are plenty of *ex*-captains of England, only one captain.

But: *le roi est mort, vive le roi*! The career of the king-designate had begun on a blessed note blossoming from its streaky start into an innings of regal bravura and panache. Botham had scored his 89 in 77 minutes off only 76 balls. The previous Saturday, on the same ground, Ian had smashed 228 in three hours. He had also finished the tour at a heroic level, scoring a century in the last Test in Australia and another in the Jubilee Test in Bombay. In the latter, he also took thirteen wickets, and indeed throughout that trip he held our bowling together. Often he and Derek Underwood had to bowl for far too long for their own interests and success, simply because they were so easily the most reliable of our bowlers. Until those last two Tests Ian's batting had been a disappointment, provoking cries of 'irresponsibility' from the critics. In the first Test, at Perth, he played with reckless fury in the first innings, enraged at what he saw as the faintheartedness of our early batsmen after he had bowled 35 overs and taken 6–78. He was right to be cross – some batsmen had looked as if they were in awe of Jeff Thomson, Dennis Lillee and the Perth pitch – but wrong to let it affect his game.

For the most part, however, Botham used his talent resourcefully; his head was only rarely over-ruled by his heart, as when he succumbed to the urge to prove a point with bouncers on a slow pitch where the odds were in the batsman's favour. He always erred on the side of attack rather than defence, and I nearly always encouraged him in this.

I had long been impressed by his natural feel for the game and by his tactical suggestions. He is generous to team-mates who have far less ability than he has and to opponents who have – on a day – got the better of him and his team. I remember his gesture in bowling a slow long-hop to Greg Chappell at Sydney when Australia needed 1 to win and Chappell needed 6 for his century (Chappell hit it first bounce for four, and ended on 98 not out).

Because of these strengths, we had appointed Botham to the tour committee. It was a close call between him and David Gower for that role, and so quite possible that, had we then given Gower this measure of responsibility, he would have been able to show qualities of leadership that would have convinced the selectors that he rather than

Botham should lead England in 1980. They are of course two very different men, Gower cool, intelligent, perceptive, subtle; Botham warm (sometimes hot), shrewd, less complicated, bold.

But that is speculation. Botham did this mainly unexacting job well. He was confident in his exercise of authority. He responded with chuckling good humour to Geoff Boycott's jibes about his stripes needing a polish, and was assured and perceptive enough to help Geoff with his batting early on. He pointed out that in trying to deal with the extra bounce of Australian pitches Boycott was becoming rooted on the back foot. The result was that he was unable to transfer any weight on to the front foot, so half volleys were not being punished, and he was static and immobile in the face of bouncers. He had in fact recently been hit on the head by the Combined Universities' opening bowler, and been hit several times on the shoulder or back by Richard Hadlee on a slow pitch in Tasmania. Botham's advice helped Boycott to take on with great success the fastest bowlers in the world over the next eighteen months.

Botham's forthright humour was nearly always productive. Occasionally the teasing would go too far. His close friend, Bob Willis, was at that time acutely aware of the fact that his body would not respond smoothly, however hard he tried. He was not always encouraged by Botham's repeatedly comparing him to a wounded camel. I, like Ian, failed to notice that Bob's sensitivity was being hurt until he told me in Bombay. When I mentioned this to Ian, he took the point. I remember, in this conversation, our talking quite openly about the possibility of his succeeding me; he was unambivalently keen to do so.

The greatest drawback in making Botham captain was his lack of experience in the job. It is hard for a young England player to be made county captain. Senior professionals often resent a younger boss. Tests deprive counties of players for almost half a season. Few potential England captains like Botham, Graham Gooch (as we thought then), or Gower get the chance to learn the job by making mistakes in the less exposed world of county cricket. And those who, perhaps by sheer luck, are given this opportunity are sometimes too enthusiastically acclaimed as potential England leaders. Geoff Miller would not have been made vice-captain when Willis flew home from the West Indies without his few weeks as Derbyshire captain. There had been talk of Roger Knight or John Barclay as candidates to lead England – premature, surely, whatever their successes at Surrey or Sussex.

In spite of his inexperience, I felt that Botham was the best bet in 1980 and wholeheartedly wished him well. Part of his appeal to me, as to others, consisted, I think, in his being so different in character from me. He is physically strong and outgoing, I am weak and comparatively introverted. He has charisma as a player, I do not. He is blunt, optimistic and young; I am more sensitive, perhaps, more pessimistic – and ageing! After Tony Greig I may have been an agreeable contrast; after me, Botham offered tremendous hope for a new, vital start. Selectors cannot but be a little influenced by and involved in a prevailing mood. The time was ripe for the rise of the Hero, someone who could inspire his team by his own performance to take on the Arch-Enemies.

For a while in the summer of 1980 things went reasonably well. But there was already a hint of Ian's bowling decline, which he dates to the onset of his back injury at Oxford in April. Certainly in our match at Taunton his pace was more gentle than it had been just a few months before at Bombay. However, he batted well in the two one-day Internationals, scoring 30 and 42 not out. Moreover, England won the second match in a roaring finish, having lost the previous one by only 24 runs. He scored a splendid 57 on a mediocre pitch in the first Test, at Nottingham, but we lost the match narrowly, by two wickets. Now his own form gradually deteriorated. He was overweight. His back was not right; I'm told that X-rays showed that the vertebrae were out of alignment. By playing he laid himself open to the criticism which his performances increasingly justified in comparison with his own past standards. I saw him bowl in the Centenary Test in August, and he was a shadow of himself.

This personal decline in batting, bowling and fielding continued through the winter and into the 1981 season at home. Quite early, as captain, he had begun to look more tense. A friend of mine glimpsed on TV a face that seemed familiar. 'There's Mike,' she thought, 'looking worried.' It was in fact Botham with that haunted, weighed-down captaincy look. In the Centenary Test I felt that he lost his nerve a little: the earlier, optimistic Botham would have leapt at the chance of having a go at Chappell's target on the last afternoon. The new pessimist preferred not to take the risk – either of another personal failure or of a struggle to save the match.

My impression is that Ian found it hard to take advice and even harder to take criticism. Before, when I was captain, I would find that his initial response to a mild criticism from me would be trenchantly opposed; but that he would in his own time often come to see my point. When *he* was captain his stubbornness encountered dangerously fewer obstacles. One England player told me that he was physically afraid to pursue a suggestion if Ian had once disagreed with it; another that he bottled up comments lest they should count against him in selection. Ian found it hard to contain divergent opinions or tolerate differences inside the team. The sharper, less kindly criticisms from outside made him boil, and he became, I think, paranoid about the media.

Nevertheless, he retained many of his strengths during a most trying tour. The side's rhythm was hampered by rain and bad practice facilities, by injury and by politics. They were above all devastated by Ken Barrington's sudden death. Throughout, they did not fall out with each other, or with the umpires, crowd or press. The atmosphere between the teams was more amicable than ever, thanks largely to Botham and his friendships with Viv Richards, Michael Holding and Joel Garner. In fact he spreads an air of camaraderie with cricketers from every country. When the going was hardest on the field, Ian himself would bowl for two hours at a time. He maintained within the side the feeling that the West Indies could be held, even beaten. He encouraged players to keep going at their natural game.

But by the beginning of the 1981 season, which followed all too hard on the heels of the West Indies tour, Ian Botham was on trial. The media entered into the spirit of it, sensing a victim. The drama of the young king's rise to the throne was matched only by the excitement of his deposition. 'For in the hollow crown that rounds the mortal temples of a king, keeps Death his court.' The BBC offered a courtroom of a particularly insidious kind in Newsnight which, during the 1981 Nottingham Test, presented the 'Trial of Ian Botham', featuring a case for the prosecution (dropped catch, out for one etc) and a somewhat silent defence.

By the end of the Lord's Test, Ian had finally had enough. Richards had said to me shortly before that Ian was too good a player to worry about the captaincy, and that it *was* a worry for him; he had seen him in the Caribbean, brooding over a drink, kidding himself that he didn't mind the criticisms. 'In one-day matches I saw him edging round the field to pick out the man who was shouting abuse at him instead of doing what you must do – put up with it.'

Ian has described how it was even harder for his wife to put up with the last months of his captaincy. 'She was pestered wherever she went,' he told me, 'when she had enough problems being by herself with the kids.' At Lord's he resigned. He felt that it had been unreasonable to be given tenure so parsimoniously, match by match. He wrote afterwards that he was in a daze during this second Test. But I think he knew, before offering his resignation, that the selectors had already decided to replace him. He received kindly and sensible advice from Bernard Thomas and, I believe, from Gubby Allen. In his final interview he admitted his worries, and showed great dignity. And as he at last emerged from the pavilion to leave with his wife, Nick Hunter, the BBC producer, helped her to avoid the photographers and some of the embarrassment of their departure.

Perhaps he was too young; too raw; perhaps he did still need a framework within which he could fully be himself, against which he could at times hit out, and from which he would receive some protection. But a similar verdict might have been passed on several other candidates for the job at that time. And my 'advice' to 'Both', in a letter I sent him while he was away, was to try captaining England against someone else! No captain can ever have had a harder task than he had in his year at the helm.

2

Australia Go One Up

Botham's first chance since the Centenary Test of captaining England against a side less awesome than the West Indies came on Thursday 18 June at Trent Bridge. This was the ground on which he had four years before made his début for England, taking 5–74 in Australia's first innings. Since 1977 the pitch at Nottingham had increasingly favoured seam-bowling. In 1980 England, like the West Indies, had gone into the game without a specialist spinner, and it was rumoured that both teams would follow this example now. I happened to know more about Australia's intentions in the matter than our own. Middlesex had played the Australians earlier in the same week, and I had chatted with Rodney Hogg and Rod Marsh after the first day's play. More open with me now that I was out of the Test scene, Hogg had hinted that they were likely to omit Ray Bright ('You don't often win a Test at Nottingham with a spinner, do you?'), while Marsh confessed that the man they would least like to see at No. 3 for England was Bob Woolmer, who was in fact named the following morning to fill this one open place in the England twelve.

At 5 a.m. on the first morning of the series, Ron Allsop, the groundsman, walked out to remove the covers and take a look at his strip. To his horror, he saw small piles of earth all round it; as he came closer, the early light revealed a couple of objects uncannily resembling moles. Poor Allsop must for a moment have wondered whether he had been reading too many articles about MI5, or if a new breed of super-mole had mutated right under his nose as he had lovingly rolled the pitch reserved and prepared each year for the Test.

First Test, Trent Bridge, 18–22 June

ENGLAND First Innings

G. A. Gooch, c Wood, b Lillee	10
G. Boycott, c Border, b Alderman	27
R. A. Woolmer, c Wood, b Lillee	0
D. I. Gower, c Yallop, b Lillee	26
M. W. Gatting, lbw, b Hogg	52
P. Willey, c Border, b Alderman	10
I. T. Botham, b Alderman	1
P. R. Downton, c Yallop, b Alderman	8
G. R. Dilley, b Hogg	34
R. G. D. Willis, c Marsh, b Hogg	0
M. Hendrick, not out	6
Extras (lb 6, w 1, nb 4)	11
TOTAL	185

Fall of Wickets: 1–13, 2–13, 3–57, 4–67, 5–92, 6–96, 7–116, 8–159, 9–159, 10–185.

Bowling: Lillee, 13–3–34–3; Alderman, 24–7–68–4; Hogg, 11.4–1–47–3; Lawson, 8–3–25–0.

Second Innings

G. A. Gooch, c Yallop, b Lillee	6
G. Boycott, c Marsh, b Alderman	4
R. A. Woolmer, c Marsh, b Alderman	0
D. I. Gower, c sub, b Lillee	28
M. W. Gatting, lbw, b Alderman	15
P. Willey, lbw, b Lillee	13
I. T. Botham, c Border, b Lillee	33
P. R. Downton, lbw, b Alderman	3
G. R. Dilley, c Marsh, b Alderman	13
R. G. D. Willis, c Chappell, b Lillee	1
M. Hendrick, not out	0
Extras (lb 8, nb 1)	9
TOTAL	125

Fall of Wickets: 1–12, 2–12, 3–13, 4–39, 5–61, 6–94, 7–109, 8–113, 9–125, 10–125.

Bowling: Lillee, 16.4–2–46–5; Alderman, 19–3–62–5; Hogg, 3–1–8–0.

AUSTRALIA First Innings

G. M. Wood, lbw, b Dilley		0
J. Dyson, c Woolmer, b Willis		5
G. N. Yallop, b Hendrick		13
K. J. Hughes, lbw, b Willis		7
T. M. Chappell, b Hendrick		17
A. R. Border, c and b Botham		63
R. W. Marsh, c Boycott, b Willis		19
G. F. Lawson, c Gower, b Botham		14
D. K. Lillee, c Downton, b Botham		12
R. M. Hogg, c Boycott, b Dilley		0
T. M. Alderman, not out		12
Extras (b 4, lb 8, w 1, nb 4)		17
TOTAL		179

Fall of Wickets: 1–0, 2–21, 3–21, 4–33, 5–64, 6–89, 7–110, 8–147, 9–153, 10–179.

Bowling: Dilley, 20–7–38–3; Willis, 30–14–47–3; Hendrick, 20–7–43–2; Botham, 16.5–6–34–2.

Second Innings

J. Dyson, c Downton, b Dilley		38
G. M. Wood, c Woolmer, b Willis		8
G. N. Yallop, c Gatting, b Botham		6
K. J. Hughes, lbw, b Dilley		22
T. M. Chappell, not out		20
A. R. Border, b Dilley		20
R. W. Marsh, lbw, b Dilley		0
G. F. Lawson, not out		5
Extras (b 1, lb 6, nb 6)		13
TOTAL (6 wkts)		132

D. K. Lillee, R. M. Hogg and T. M. Alderman did not bat.

Fall of Wickets: 1–20, 2–40, 3–77, 4–80, 5–122, 6–122.

Bowling: Dilley, 11.1–4–24–4; Willis, 13–2–28–1; Hendrick, 20–7–33–0; Botham, 10–1–34–1.

Umpires: W. E. Alley and D. J. Constant.

Australia won by 4 wkts.

The moles were real enough, but long dead and planted with their 'hills' by a practical joker on the Notts staff (not, I should say, to head off one possible line of speculation, by Derek Randall, though it was he who told me the story). However, other anxieties about the pitch were not so quickly removed. Any slight chance that either John Emburey or Bright would be included was ruled out by the cold, cloudy weather. Kim Hughes won the toss and put England in to bat.

It was as clear from the score-card as from the television highlights (which were all that I could see of the first two days' play, since Middlesex had a county match against Essex at Ilford) that seam-bowling thrived. By the end of the second day, in reply to England's 185 all out, Australia had struggled to 166–9. Batting was something of a lottery, though several batsmen coped well, Mike Gatting and Allan Border each completing half-centuries that were worth double in normal conditions. More unorthodox batting methods also flourished briefly, notably Dilley's and Marsh's.

On the Saturday Middlesex had no match so I drove to Nottingham to report for the *Sunday Times*. Before play I went out to the middle to have a look at the pitch for myself. Allsop is a friendly man, always keen to hear players' views. In reply to his question, I told him my opinion: that while the pitch looked flat and whitish, the matt of grass was unusually thick. He said that he might have got it wrong, but would not stop trying to find pace and bounce to encourage attacking batting – as well as bowling – at Trent Bridge.

As he spoke, someone shouted to us to watch out; I looked up just in time to see a ball whizzing over our heads from the direction of the nets, which lie beyond the playing area at the far end of the ground. The culprit was Botham, who had struck an enormous off-drive – an obvious warning not to queer his pitch! He waved to us both merrily.

As the third day's play began it soon became clear that

the character of the pitch had not changed. Bowlers could count on one or two balls each over deviating alarmingly off the seam, and they were further aided by the variation in bounce. Even Border was beaten once or twice an over, especially by Willis, as Australia's last pair inched their way towards England's total. Finally, after nearly 4½ hours at the crease, Border was caught and bowled by Botham for 63, as he came down the wicket to drive, and Australia were all out 6 runs behind.

When England batted, I had my first chance to see Terry Alderman bowl in the flesh since 1979, when he had caused us problems on a Perth wicket not unlike the current Test pitch. On that occasion we had won the match by 140 runs despite scoring only 270 in two complete innings ourselves. Botham and Mike Hendrick had each taken eight wickets, Alderman five. Now the Australian looked the most dangerous of the three, with his long but comfortable run-up. His body does not lean back in delivery, but, with his high arm and steady head, he bowls an excellent line. As Marsh had told me at Lord's, he hits the seam more often than any of their bowlers. He also bowls a somewhat fuller length than many of his type.

No doubt he has, during his years in the Western Australia eleven, learned a great deal from his present opening partner, Lillee, who now struck the first blow by having Gooch brilliantly caught in the gully by Graham Yallop. Although wickets fell at regular intervals to one or other of the pair, none of the England batsmen let himself down. Geoff Boycott and Gower shaped well, as in the first innings, while Gooch and Peter Willey were sensibly aggressive in their own unique ways. Gatting, continuing on Saturday where he had left off on Thursday, looked the best of all. He let the ball go with fine judgment outside the off-stump, but never became obsessed with defence, punishing anything over- or under-pitched with meaty drives, cuts and hooks. Poor Woolmer got a pair without playing a single bad stroke.

In the first innings he was out to a nasty lifter from Lillee; in the second he edged a beauty from Alderman that set off towards middle-and-leg then veered sharply towards the slips. Cricket can be cruel.

Botham too had been feeling its sting. In the first two days little had gone right for him. He was out for one, playing across the line, and took only one wicket. Worse still, he missed two chances at slip, part of the rash of dropped catches that without doubt cost England the match. On the third day he came in with the score at 61–5 and proceeded to play sensibly and well, letting loose some cracking off-drives against the tiring Alderman. When play was stopped – for the day as it turned out – because of bad light and rain, England very much depended on their captain to rescue them from the precarious position of being only 100 runs ahead with four wickets in hand.

The fourth – and last – day was the first Sunday on which Test cricket had been played in England. Personally, I am not against Sunday play, but I do think it wrong to stage Test matches without a rest day at all. After three days the players and umpires need a break, for relaxation and to give themselves an opportunity to recover from aches and pains. The day off should come at this point, as in an average five-day match the first two innings (but not the third) should be completed by then. At Trent Bridge the low scores meant that the lack of a rest day was no hardship to anyone; in fact, on the contrary, everyone was pleased not to have the flow of the game interrupted by an empty day.

Perhaps the Australians' prayers were answered. They must at least have been pleased at the change in the weather, for on Sunday the sun shone for almost the first time in the match. Border caught a fine low catch at second slip to get rid of Botham, and England's last four wickets fell for 31, leaving Australia 132 to win. They scrambled home by four wickets despite a late burst of excitement when Dilley took two wickets with the score on 122.

My overall impression of the match was that England batted and bowled at least as well as Australia; the one difference lay in the close catching. The Australians missed only one chance throughout, while we dropped no less than six relatively easy catches in the first innings, which allowed the visitors to recover from 33–4 on the first evening to come within reach of our first-innings score. They then rubbed salt into the wound, and tilted the match their way, with some brilliant catches in the second innings. Yallop's (already referred to) and Martin Kent's (to dismiss Gower, at fourth slip) were remarkable in any conditions, let alone the chilly gloom in which most of this match was fought out. In each case the ball was travelling not only fast but wide of the fielder; in such cold conditions, eye and fingers have no right to co-ordinate so perfectly. There is little to be done about the days when a team acts like a single jittery individual and puts down chance after chance. Indeed, on the same ground almost a year before the Australians themselves had dropped fourteen in their game against Notts. They either stick or they don't. A captain can merely hope that his hunches about the most likely fielders to hold the slip-catches are sound, and try not to change the combination too often. Towards the end of Australia's first innings, for example, I was surprised to see Dilley at third slip, for he usually fields in the deep and Gatting was available for the slips.

If the unfavourable balance of slip-catching cost England the match, it had longer-term consequences as well. For one thing, I should not now be polishing up this manuscript as the sun sets behind the trees in Ahmedabad and the parrots flash screeching by. If England had won the first Test, Botham would almost certainly have been appointed for the rest of the series. It is possible, too, that just one missed chance cost Paul Downton his place. He had by all accounts kept excellently in the West Indies, and ended the tour with a stubborn innings in the last Test. At home, he had not been at his best, but would I think have been retained if he had not dropped a 'sitter' from Border when he had scored only 10; as luck would have it, Border's innings was the crucial one, so Downton's error became more noteworthy. Hendrick, who bowled the ball that Border edged and Downton dropped, no doubt remembers it too, and his Test career might have bloomed for longer. The precariousness of cricket is shown even more concretely by the subsequent fate of Downton and four of his tour colleagues: before the end of the 1981 season, Downton, Dilley, Roland Butcher, Bill Athey and Graham Stevenson had all lost not only their Test but their county places.

Ian Botham could scarcely be blamed for England's defeat. I was, however, struck by two aspects of his performance as captain. The first concerned bowling changes. Australia's first innings took place in conditions in which, at almost every other time in Botham's career, his captain would virtually have had to prise the ball from his grip in order to take him off. Yet it was not until the 54th over that he put himself on. This reticence, which may have been caused in part by past criticism that he had at times bowled himself too much, was not necessarily bad captaincy (though it is always a risk in having a front-line bowler as captain that he himself may bowl either too little or too much). But it was a telling indication of his loss of confidence in himself. Second, some of his remarkable buoyancy was lacking. The Nottingham crowd supported him warmly throughout; he was relaxed and philosophical in his TV interview at the end of the match. Yet when Geoff Lawson chipped a Botham half-volley to Gower at cover to give Ian his first wicket there was none of the radiant grin of the man who basks in expected good fortune. I have never seen Ian come closer to looking apologetic about taking a wicket.

The man of the match award went, remarkably, to D. K. Lillee. There is nothing unusual in his being the outstanding player in any game in which he participates.

What made this particular achievement so incredible and admirable was that Dennis had contracted viral pneumonia early in May, and was still far from being fully fit. To my mind it was only in the sixth Test, at the end of August, that he was able to bowl with the sustained fire and accuracy of the man who has for a decade been the best bowler in the world.

Many of Lillee's successes for Australia came when he was the single spearhead of the attack. Since 1974, however, he has for much of the time had the support of a genuinely fast bowler, either Jeff Thomson or Len Pascoe. When the team to tour England was announced in March, both these names were, for different reasons, missing from it. Pascoe we knew was unavailable, as he needed an operation on his knee; his unfitness made the omission of Thomson, who had had a good season for Queensland, even more surprising. It was unusual for Australia to tour England with only one specialist spinner. I would have expected either Bruce Yardley, the off-spinner and hard-hitting batsman, or Jim Higgs, the leg-spinner, to have accompanied Bright.

Of even more significance was the absence of Greg Chappell, who had decided to stay at home for personal and business reasons. Chappell had for some years been unhappy about the frequency and length of overseas tours. The problem of a successor must have been far from easy. Hughes, who had captained Australia in India towards the end of the Packer era (taking over from Yallop), and had been Chappell's vice-captain, was likeable and straightforward. But he was young and, perhaps revealingly fresh-faced; would he have the toughness and tactical sharpness to win over Marsh and Lillee? Marsh himself was the rival candidate. He is an astute thinker about the game, and had been highly respected as captain of Western Australia both before and after his absence with Packer. For many years he had been both Ian Chappell's and Greg's lieutenant. Under a man of Greg's stature the disrespect between players that had marred the Packer period must have been healed or at least papered over; could the cracks reappear with a new leader? Hughes, the Establishment's choice, might, one felt, have a difficult time ahead with his senior pros.

This backward glance permits a digression to explain how Thomson joined Middlesex in April 1981, and to give a brief account of his – and my – confrontation with the Australians for the county just before the first Test. In March, I had awaited the announcement of the Australian team with more than usual interest. Middlesex needed a fast bowler to take the place of Vintcent van der Bijl, the big South African who had done so well for us in 1980. We had failed to persuade van der Bijl to return, even for a few weeks at the start of the season so that he could play for us during the university term, before Simon Hughes came down from Durham. We knew that it was likely that Emburey, and possible that Phil Edmonds, would be involved in the summer's Tests; if a Middlesex player were to be picked for all six Tests and the three one-day Internationals he would, we counted, miss no less than thirteen of our twenty-two championship matches. Our reserve strength was raw. We had to do our best to find another experienced bowler. We would want him to do the job for one season only, because in 1982 new rules would restrict counties to one overseas player in any one match, and our plans were that Wayne Daniel should continue to fill that role.

Our requirements, therefore, were stringent. We would seek to sign a world-class performer. We had no interest in having on our staff an overseas player who was only marginally better than our own, nor would we have time, in a single season, to develop unproved potential, however great. We had already made enquiries of Kapil Dev, the Indian all-rounder, but his extreme elusiveness suggested to us at best an ambivalent interest. We had shown a tentative but, as it proved, abortive interest in Colin Croft. I had also phoned Adelaide, to seek the advice of John Inverarity, who was

still playing Sheffield Shield cricket. Apart from those
who were likely to come to England he mentioned one
Alderman; I am afraid that my response was that I would
find it hard to recommend him wholeheartedly to the
Middlesex committee as he could hardly at that time be
described as a 'world-class' bowler. Outside Australia
there was no one who seemed entirely suitable. We
would have to see who was not selected for the tour.

After the announcement I phoned Greg Chappell in
Brisbane. Why, I wondered, had Thommo been omitted?
Should we consider anyone else – Geoff Dymock,
perhaps, or Max Walker? Chappell told me that Walker's
knees were causing him more and more trouble, and that
Thomson had bowled much better for Queensland than
Dymock. He had in fact been the second-highest wicket-
taker in Shield Cricket that season, bowling extremely
fast at times even on easy-paced pitches. Greg thought
that county cricket might suit Thommo; he has always
got himself match-fit by bowling, but has never enjoyed
net practice, so the more continuous cricket in England
might help him. The main question mark concerned his
motivation: Jeff appeared to be torn between the desire to
bowl fast and the wish to go fishing; or, rather, the
ambition to buy an ocean-going boat which he could use
to make a living by taking others on fishing trips.
Interestingly, both Chappell and Inverarity mentioned
Mike Whitney, the young left-arm quickie from New
South Wales, as the best long-term prospect in Australia.

Thomson was keen. The boat-purchase had fallen
through. He was tickled by the idea of being able to prove
a point to the Australian selectors, and wanted to play in
London for Middlesex.

So it came about that Thomson and Lillee came
separately to England, practised separately, but drank,
when they had the chance, together. They also caught
'flu at about the same time; but though Thomson's was
bad enough, it was not as serious as the pneumonia
which laid Lillee low. The weather in May was so wet that

neither of them missed a great deal of cricket, and the Australian team's preparations for the important matches were badly hampered by rain. When the one-day Internationals were played early in June, none of their batsmen had found much form; Lillee, though nowhere near fit, played. The press, predictably, described the tourists as the weakest Australian team ever. Equally predictably, the Australians proved them wrong.

One-day Internationals are a curious feature of a tour. They excite attention, and produce much good cricket. Performances in them can affect selection for the Test matches. They seem important at the time, but in the assessment of a tour they count for nothing. Who will remember, in years to come, that in 1981 Australia won the Prudential Trophy by two matches to one? For the record then: England won the first match at Lord's by the comfortable margin of six wickets. Australia won the second at Birmingham by 2 runs, thanks to brilliant catches near the end by Hughes and Geoff Lawson. And Australia won the third, at Headingley, handsomely, scoring 236–8 on an awkward pitch and proceeding to bowl much better to limit England to only 165–9.

Meanwhile, for Middlesex, Thomson had recovered and bowled very fast against Somerset. Four days later came the confrontation to which he, and we, had been looking forward: Middlesex v. the Australians at Lord's. It was my first chance to see the tourists at close quarters; I expected it also to be my last. As it was the match before the first Test, they paid us the compliment of picking virtually their strongest side. Only Alderman was missing from the twelve for Trent Bridge. Middlesex, too, fielded a team of internationals, our latest cap being Butcher who had played in three Tests in the Caribbean.

The weather was, at last, perfect for cricket, but the pitch had not dried as fast as the groundsman expected, so it was a good toss for the Australians to win; they asked us to bat first. As Lillee was about to deliver his first ball, someone made a slight movement behind the arm and Graham Barlow stepped back, causing Dennis to limp to a halt, cursing. This prompted Marsh to request him sarcastically not to move his arms about so much as he ran in to bowl. Ironically, it was Barlow who pulled a muscle an hour later, and was unfit for a fortnight. Lillee took a couple of overs to find his rhythm. Knowing that the pitch would be slow, I twice hooked him, but nearly gloved another short delivery that bounced like a tennis ball. I did not last long, though, for as soon as Lillee found his length he nipped one back from off to have me LBW. He bowled the right pace to get movement from this pitch, but it was hard to form an opinion about his fitness.

We did well to lose only two wickets by lunch, but collapsed to a mixture of wild shots and good balls after the interval. We feared that 150 would be a paltry score on the, by now, benign pitch, but over the next four hours all our bowlers were near their best. Thomson hit Graeme Wood on the cheek when the batsman changed his mind about hooking; fortunately the injury was not serious, though he needed an X-ray to make sure. Remembering all those fiery quotes from Thomson to the effect that he hated batsmen and aimed to hit, I was interested to notice that he was visibly upset by this injury and not only, as cynics might have it, because Wood was a fellow-countryman. Many fast bowlers are less bloodthirsty than they would have you believe.

Overnight, the tourists were 69–2; and we had dropped Hughes twice in the slips. Next day, Thomson, bowling at top pace, took two early wickets. The other wickets were shared, and, amazingly, we had a lead of 4 runs, which we extended to about 100 for the loss of two wickets by close of play. Middlesex had played Oxford University over the three days preceding this match; I had not played, preferring to spend some time in the indoor cricket school at Lord's, where my batting was filmed and replayed by video. I find it most useful to check my technique periodically in this way, and the result was that in the middle I felt steadier at the crease and better balanced than at any time since the previous summer. Next day I reached 100, my second against the Australians (the first, also for Middlesex, being way back in 1964). Although Lillee was unable to generate much pace, Rodney Hogg bowled a few really quick deliveries, and Lawson showed his versatility with the odd leg-cutter and off-cutter. Bright wheeled away accurately, but I found him much easier to cope with bowling round the wicket in the orthodox fashion. He had not yet settled upon over the wicket as his stock method.

A three-day match on so gentle a pitch was always likely to be a draw, though we did give ourselves a smattering of hope by taking three early wickets in their second innings. However, John Dyson and Yallop played the spinners safely, and the match ended quietly with a few leg-breaks from Thomson.

It was a pleasure to play against the Australians without all the tension and bristle of a Test. The game was serious enough, but there was room for the occasional comment or conversation. At one point I lost a screw from my helmet on the field; during the interval, Marsh brought a spare to our dressing-room. Earlier, Hughes told Hogg, who was at mid-on with no mid-wicket or square-leg, to watch out for the single. Hogg nodded, then drily remarked that a fellow can't cover the entire leg-side. I had read that Hogg had captained South Australia the previous winter. I asked him what he thought of the job and if he had any tips. He said he did it for only one match, against the Indians; he had a 100% record, but in the first innings, when India scored over 400, he found his team-mates edging away from him when he approached them for advice. 'In the second,' he added, 'India collapsed and were all out for about 70; the entire team were coming up to me with tactical ideas then!'

On the evidence of this match Thommo had indeed

been unlucky to be left out, as he was quicker than any of their bowlers, and as accurate. Nevertheless, even without him, they were clearly a stronger bowling than batting side; Chappell T. was no replacement for Chappell G. All the early batsmen had looked vulnerable against the pace of Thomson and Daniel; Hughes, who was having a rough patch, in particular. It was salutary to be reminded, by Hogg again, that Hughes's Test average was 43, compared with a career average of 33. And it was unlikely that England's attack would be as penetrating as ours. Certainly from the Middlesex point of view the match was encouraging, though we knew that from now on we were likely to lose Emburey and Gatting for most of our matches. We could not know that Thomson's days of cricket that summer were numbered. He was already feeling a lump near his solar plexus which he simply – and characteristically – pushed back in. Next week a specialist told him on no account to play cricket again until he had had an operation for a herniated intestine. We had seen enough to know that Jeff was a great trier, who encouraged the younger players (notably Wilf Slack, who did so well in July and August). Thommo was the first, at middle practice, to help out by fetching balls from all corners of the ground. Like many great cricketers, he sets himself the highest standards; once, after a marvellous opening spell that left him panting for breath, he apologised for a couple of wasted deliveries.

By the time the second Test began, on 2 July, Thomson had already had his operation and was out of hospital. Hogg was again having trouble with his back – there was talk of Greg Chappell replacing him if he failed a fitness test – so Bright took his place at Lord's. England made two changes: the effervescent Bob Taylor, still as fit as ever at 39, came in for Downton, and Emburey for Hendrick.

I saw even less of this match than of the first Test. It seems to have been an uneven game, with mixed weather and mixed fortunes, ending fairly enough as a

Second Test, Lords, 2–7 July

ENGLAND First Innings

G. A. Gooch, c Yallop, b Lawson	44
G. Boycott, c Alderman, b Lawson	17
R. A. Woolmer, c Marsh, b Lawson	21
D. I. Gower, c Marsh, b Lawson	27
M. W. Gatting, lbw, b Bright	59
P. Willey, c Border, b Alderman	82
J. E. Emburey, run out	31
I. T. Botham, lbw, b Lawson	0
R. W. Taylor, c Hughes, b Lawson	0
G. R. Dilley, not out	7
R. G. D. Willis, c Wood, b Lawson	5
Extras (b 2, lb 3, w 3, nb 10)	18
TOTAL	311

Fall of Wickets: 1–60, 2–65, 3–134, 4–187, 5–284, 6–293, 7–293, 8–293, 9–298, 10–311.

Bowling: Lillee, 35.4–7–102–0;
Alderman, 30.2–7–79–1;
Lawson, 43.1–14–81–7; Bright, 15–7–31–1.

Second Innings

G. A. Gooch, lbw, b Lawson	20
G. Boycott, c Marsh, b Lillee	60
R. A. Woolmer, lbw, b Alderman	9
D. I. Gower, c Alderman, b Lillee	89
M. W. Gatting, c Wood, b Bright	16
I. T. Botham, b Bright	0
P. Willey, c Chappell, b Bright	12
G. R. Dilley, not out	27
R. W. Taylor, b Lillee	9
Extras (b 2, lb 8, nb 13)	23
TOTAL (8 wkts dec)	265

J. E. Emburey and R. G. D. Willis did not bat.

Fall of Wickets: 1–31, 2–55, 3–178, 4–217, 5–217, 6–217, 7–242, 8–265.

Bowling: Lillee, 26.4–8–82–3;
Alderman, 17–2–42–1; Lawson, 19–6–51–1;
Bright, 36–18–67–3.

AUSTRALIA First Innings

G. M. Wood, c Taylor, b Willis	44
J. Dyson, c Gower, b Botham	7
G. N. Yallop, b Dilley	1
K. J. Hughes, c Willis, b Emburey	42
T. M. Chappell, c Taylor, b Dilley	2
A. R. Border, c Gatting, b Botham	64
R. W. Marsh, lbw, b Dilley	47
R. J. Bright, lbw, b Emburey	33
G. F. Lawson, lbw, b Willis	5
D. K. Lillee, not out	40
T. M. Alderman, c Taylor, b Willis	5
Extras (b 6, lb 11, w 6, nb 32)	55
TOTAL	345

Fall of Wickets: 1–62, 2–62, 3–69, 4–81,
5–167, 6–244, 7–257, 8–268, 9–314, 10–345.

Bowling: Willis, 27.4–9–50–3;
Dilley, 30–8–106–3; Botham, 26–8–71–2;
Gooch, 10–4–28–0; Emburey, 25–12–35–2.

Second Innings

G. M. Wood, not out	62
J. Dyson, lbw, b Dilley	1
G. N. Yallop, c Botham, b Willis	3
K. J. Hughes, lbw, b Dilley	4
T. M. Chappell, c Taylor, b Botham	5
A. R. Border, not out	12
Extras (w 1, nb 2)	3
TOTAL (4 wkts)	90

R. W. Marsh, R. J. Bright,
G. F. Lawson, D. K. Lillee and
T. M. Alderman did not bat.

Fall of Wickets: 1–2, 2–11, 3–17, 4–62.

Bowling: Willis, 12–3–35–1;
Dilley, 7.5–1–18–2; Emburey, 21–10–24–0;
Botham, 8–3–10–1.

Umpires: D. O. Oslear and K. E. Palmer.   **Match drawn.**

draw. In his hundredth Test, Boycott looked set for a hundred of his own, but fell to Marsh and Lillee. It was Lillee's, and Taylor's, first Test as MBES. Lawson, in his third Test, produced a prodigious effort to take 7–81 in England's first innings, while in Botham's twelfth as captain he was out for a pair.

Hughes won the toss again, and once again put England in. Perhaps he was influenced by the movement his bowlers had found against Middlesex on the first morning, but the Test pitch looked dry. After an hour, in which Gooch played with control and power, Hughes must have regretted his decision. Lawson, however, caused all sorts of problems in a few fast overs in which he dismissed both Gooch and Boycott and caused Woolmer to retire hurt after being hit full on the forearm. When he bowled from the Pavilion End he found traditional help from the Lord's ridge, which is exactly on a fast bowler's length. If the ball lands on its upward slope it rises sharply, while it can also keep low if pitched only a couple of feet further up. Otherwise the pitch was firm and true.

Gatting, first with Gower and then with Willey, was for the second consecutive Test the pick of England's batsmen, but again contrived to get out in his 50s. This time he had only himself to blame, playing lazily neither forward nor back to Bright. Having survived Lawson's marathon spell – he bowled 22 consecutive overs, and still had the energy for a few more at the end – and having seen Alderman limp off with a strained hamstring in midafternoon, Gatting must have fancied his chances of that elusive maiden Test century. His dismissal – for 59 – ten minutes before the close brought Australia back almost to even terms with the score 191–4 at stumps.

Friday was an unhappy day, starting with showers and ending with sunshine and controversy. In between, Willey and Emburey ground their side to a position of near-impregnability, but then England threw away much of this advantage by losing their last six wickets for 27.

Willey's was a typically tenacious innings. He defended resolutely for much of the time, and had some trouble with Alderman's away-swingers from the Nursery End; but whenever the opportunity arose he struck the ball powerfully through the covers. Alderman, his thigh tightly strapped, was well below full pace, but kept going. I was surprised to see Lillee given the Pavilion End and Lawson the less helpful Nursery End at the start of the day; later Lawson again bowled splendidly towards the ridge, and picked up four more wickets as just reward for another excellent day's work. For three hours, however, Australia could not penetrate the rock-like immobility of the night-watchman Emburey, and his partnership with Willey took the score to 284–4. Emburey is a curiously static batsman, who lifts his bat up less than any player I know, but keeps it straight in defence. When he had a short partnership with Thomson at Headingley early in May, it was as if we had a typhoon at one end and a dead calm at the other. I think John was beginning to feel embarrassed about the length of his stay when he fell to an old trick by the artful Lillee, who had, as usual, been signing autographs and eating bananas down at fine leg. His air of distraction lured Emburey to attempt a fatal second run for a leg-glance off Lawson. Lillee surprised him with his speed on to the ball and his hard, accurate throw. The collapse followed, and England were all out for 311.

The controversy occurred when, during the extra hour which was added on to make up some of the time lost earlier in the day, the umpires came off for bad light. Soon afterwards the sun shone brightly, and the crowd, understandably, were at a loss to know why there was no play. There was a barrage of cushions from irate and perplexed spectators. Apparently the umpires were under the mistaken impression that any break during the extra hour meant the end of play for the day, and had told the players so; the Australian opening batsmen were therefore happily in the bath when the light improved.

The third day was both more interesting and more satisfactory, ending once again with the match on an even keel. Australia played enterprisingly, scoring 253–6 off 79 overs. Wood, as Gooch had done for England, got them off to a racing start, 50 coming up in only the eighth over, though he was lucky that the ball which he edged to Woolmer at short-leg turned out to be one of Willis's numerous no-balls. However, a brilliant catch by Taylor that went fast and low off Wood's inside edge started a sudden rattle of wickets. Dilley, Willis and Botham all looked impressive as four fell for only 19 runs; the Australians must have been glad of the break when lunch came with the score 81–4.

Afterwards, Hughes and Border played very well, Border pulling Botham for two fours and a six. They had taken the score to 167 when, from Emburey's third ball of the innings, Hughes had one of his rushes of blood. He skied it high over mid-off, where the spidery Willis misjudged the awkward catch, then did well to cling on to it above his head. Marsh now also played at his best, forcing Emburey square on the off-side for several fours. It took a brilliant catch by Gatting off Botham to gain England their only other wicket, Border going for 64. Marsh was 43 not out at the close, with Australia 58 runs behind with four wickets left.

Over the last two days neither side was able to establish a definite advantage. England were relieved to get Marsh in the first over with the new ball, Dilley swinging one in sharply to have him LBW without offering a stroke. He had added only 4 to his overnight score. But the Australian tail hit effectively, Bright scoring 33 and Lillee 40 not out. The last pair added an irritating 31 to give Australia a lead of 34.

An Australian win was still a possibility, so England were entirely justified in playing carefully, especially after Gooch, who had again shaped well, went at 31. Woolmer, whose arm was still uncomfortable, found the going hard, and was LBW to Alderman for 9 with the score on 55–2. We were only 21 runs ahead; and Gower faced some awkward deliveries from Lawson from one end and the prospect of Bright turning the ball sharply from the rough at the other. Boycott, however, sensibly took most of Bright's bowling. (Could not Hughes have engineered a few singles to keep them at the other ends?) It was now that Bright started to bowl over the wicket to the right-handers, too; a ploy he was to rely on for most of the remaining Tests. By the close, Boycott and Gower were still together with the score 129–2, a lead of 95.

Most of the interest in the last day's play centred on the extent to which the spinners could exploit the marks made by the bowlers' follow-throughs at the Pavilion End. This rough was likely to make life especially difficult for left-handed batsmen and especially helpful for the left-arm spinner, who could pitch the ball wider of the stumps than the off-spinner and still hit them. England advanced laboriously until lunch in the face of some accurate bowling, losing Boycott for 60. At this stage Botham clearly ordered a change of policy, and several players sacrificed their wickets going for quick runs. Botham himself was out first ball, bowled behind his legs, sweeping at Bright. There was a pointed silence as he walked up between the members after his second nought of the match.

His declaration left Australia 232 to win in a little under two hours plus twenty overs. I doubt if they ever considered going for the target; if they did, the idea was quickly destroyed when they lost three wickets to Dilley and Willis for only 17. Dilley was again inaccurate, but bowled some dangerous balls in between. Chappell hung on for an hour for 5, before being dismissed by Botham. Emburey posed problems, but did not bowl quite often enough exactly the right length or line; so Wood and Border saw Australia to safety.

Shortly after the game Ian Botham gave a second interview on television. He announced that he was not prepared to carry on as captain on a one-match basis. He thought that arrangement unfair on himself and on the side. He would be willing to carry on if he was appointed for the rest of the series. If the change came, he would be more than happy to play under anyone else; and he would prefer that someone else to be me. 'It would be better for all of us if the ship were more stable.'

Soon Alec Bedser too made a statement. He revealed that the selectors had already decided on a change. They felt that Ian was improving as a captain, but had had a rough time. They were mainly worried about his own form, though they were sure it would return. 'Ian?' he said. 'You couldn't have a better fellow.'

3

Ready for the Call

Blissfully unaware of the abdication drama four miles away, I was lying in the garden of our flat at Highgate enjoying the sun. It was still hot, and I had just retired from a stint of bowling at Mischa, aged five. On days off, especially in the middle of the season, I prefer to keep away from organised cricket, but I had looked in at Lord's before lunch to have a drink with Hogg. He had been unable to join Thomson and Downton for dinner the previous night, and Thommo had told me that Hogg would be sent home if he failed his fitness test on the Tuesday.

Thommo, Hogg, Downton and I made, it occurred to me, a quartet which might conceivably have been performing in the current Test. Hogg's try-out was more extensive than I'd realised, three separate seven-over spells in the nets. I caught him, dripping sweat outside the dressing-room, between the second and third of his spells, confident now that his back would hold out. He asked me if I had a chance of a game against them. I said I doubted it, unless they called me back as captain. I told him my fantasy, for the past year, which had been that I would score so many runs that the selectors could not fail to pick me – solely as a batsman. The fantasy went on to portray me taking century after century off Messrs Lillee, Hogg & Co.

My first intimation that something was afoot came around 8 o'clock when I had a phone call from the sports editor of the *Daily Express*. He said that they were all running round frantically, and asked if I'd heard anything. I had no idea what he was talking about, so he told me that Ian had resigned and that there were two clues about his successor: first, his selection was not dependent on availability for India and, second, as he was travelling between matches he had not yet been contacted. I said, 'I've been here for days, so it must be Keith Fletcher' (who would have been on his way home from Birmingham).

However, rumours often tell only part of the truth and that darkly; I had time to consider both alternatives. I had already, earlier, been sounded out. As the first Test was drawing to a close on the Sunday, Alan Burridge, the Middlesex secretary, asked for a quiet word with me on the balcony of the dressing room at Lord's, shortly before the start of our Sunday League match against Leicestershire. Burridge told me that Bedser wanted to know if I would be willing to take the job if asked. I had said yes. The rumour had also reached me that the selectors had actually decided to have me as captain for Lord's, then changed their minds. A leak had caused one newspaper to set up its blocks with that story; which had to be changed at the last minute. So I felt that it would have been inconsistent if the selectors now changed the captain but went for someone other than me.

Tantalised by the phone call from the *Express*, I wondered if Bedser would ring to let me know the decision. My mind raced this way and that as I accustomed myself to the anxieties attaching to the satisfaction of this newly-provoked wish, as well as to the quieter consolations of disappointment.

Half an hour later, Bedser phoned from a pub on his way home. Almost at once he was cut off; he couldn't get the coins in the box. This happened several times. At last a clear voice came through. It was the operator asking me if I would pay for the call. I said I would, and at last Alec came on the line. He said, 'We'd like you to captain the side for the rest of the series.' My first thought was, so the selectors have not been inconsistent! And there was a thrill of spurious, short-lived excitement at being, again, in the public eye. I was flattered to be asked, but also nervous. It was *my* insecurity, not the selectors' indecisiveness, that led to my appointment being for three Tests only. I suggested this at once, and Bedser accepted. I was afraid that if everything went dreadfully wrong I would not want to drag out my captaincy beyond what was welcome to the players or tolerable to me. By the sixth Test, it seemed to me, everyone might find a new face a relief. At that time I also felt that if all went amazingly well, and we had clinched the series before the Oval Test, there would be a strong case for trying out the tour captain. In the event, when that situation did arise, I was keen to have the honours of the final Test, and the chance to make the series resoundingly ours.

On the evening of 7 July the sixth Test was, of course, hidden in the future. Alec's phone call nevertheless released a flurry of emotions. About my positive response there was no real doubt: of course I would take the job – and I started to think about the practical implications straightaway. At the same time I had mixed feelings. Excitement there may have been, but stepping into a position of public prominence implied also an unwelcome loss of privacy. I had to adjust myself once again to the prospect of exposure to public questioning and criticism, to the microscopic eye of television and the trenchant views of the masses. Nor was Leeds the most propitious ground for my recall. It was indeed the ground on which we won back the Ashes in 1977, but with the bat I had a dismal Test record there, with two ducks in three innings, and yet another nought in the only one-day International I had played at the ground.

For this reason, and for others, I am hardly the darling of the Yorkshire crowds. A Headingley wag once shouted, 'There's no need to think yourself so clever, Brearley, just because you wear socks!' I wondered how many would feel that Boycott had once more been denied due recognition, and that I had been brought back solely

because of the advantages of a university career and a southern accent. As Boycott himself wrote recently, 'England seem to have a fixation with so-called leadership qualities – and it has usually meant background.' Even John Woodcock of *The Times* had been advocating Boycott's elevation. What would be the opinion of readers of the *Yorkshire Post*?

A comment of Woodcock's has often come back to me when I think about the question of fame. In 1977 he sent a report from Pakistan in which he criticised the players – fairly, I think – for not signing autographs during a long wait at Multan airport. He went on to speculate on how many of that team would still be asked for their autographs in a couple of years' time, and implied that we would look back with fondness on the days of notoriety. For myself, I never believed that I would regret the slide into anonymity. I dislike being pointed out in the street, or interrupted in a restaurant. I do not like having a pile of mail waiting for me in the Middlesex office. I do enjoy having a car lent to me – though I've always shied at the idea of having my name plastered over it (Talbots deserve a little free publicity, as for three years they provided me with a car that did not advertise its driver.) On the whole I have no interest in offering my views on TV, appearing in quiz shows, speaking at dinners, or opening bazaars. I like writing about cricket, when I have something to say, and can say it in my own way.

So much for some of my early reactions. But was I thoroughly ready for this recall? I think it worth taking space to describe my life during the precious couple of years. It is rarely appreciated that captaincy, like batting or bowling, is to an extent a matter of form. My own form went through various vicissitudes. During my last period as England captain, for example, I had had a hard time.

The tour of Australia in 1979–80 had offered me a bellyful of publicity. I was seen by the man in the Sydney street as the embodiment of all that's bad in the British. I wore my sweater over my bottom for a start, and that proved I was a 'poofter': you don't see Lillee or Thomson hiding the male hammer, do you? I talked too much, too glibly, and with the wrong accent. And when they had a go at me on the field, I *ignored* them, like the stuffy stuck-up Pom that I no doubt was. Peter McFarlane in the Melbourne *Age* informed his readers that Boycott and I were the dullest members of the touring team, the least fun of an evening. Well, you'd know that without being told, wouldn't you? That beard, too, with the ridiculous little MCC cap stuck on the top. 'Ayatollah' – foreign, archaic, puzzling – summed it up.

I also took the brunt of the hostility directed in the aftermath of Packer's World Series Cricket against the reactionary, recalcitrant Poms for refusing to go along with the new, dazzling, brash, Ocker package. Unfortunately, the playing conditions for the tour had not been finalised when we arrived in Australia. The Australian board, rightly desperate to reach a settlement with Packer which would enable all cricketers to be available for Tests, had been forced to agree to innovations, many of which they found irksome and undesirable. However, since no one, not even Packer, could force Australia's *opponents* to accept the novelties, and since opponents (and especially England) were needed for there to be a series to televise, the board could bind itself only to 'use its best endeavours' to persuade us (and others) to 'play ball'.

Now, there were those on the board who hoped privately that we would be stubborn, but not so stubborn that the series be scrapped. Then they would get their Anglo-Australian Tests (and revenues), Channel 9 would get its screens filled cheaply day after day, and we (the English) would get the blame. And that is exactly what happened.

The TCCB (Test and County Cricket Board, which runs first-class cricket in England) refused to put the Ashes at stake, arguing that the tour's format would not allow adequate preparation for Test matches. They felt, too, that a series of three matches was too short, both as a precedent and as a true battleground, for the Ashes. Ironically, my own instinct before the tour was that the Ashes should be at stake, though I felt increasingly bloodyminded in face of what I saw as Australian intransigence on other matters. Yet when we arrived, I was identified as the instigator of this pusillanimous refusal.

The TCCB had already negotiated to have the one-day triangular competition cut from five preliminary matches between each country to three, and the finals from best of five to best of three. They had expressed doubts about striped uniforms, and about white balls in matches played without lights. They had disagreed about circles for limited-overs matches (we had never played with this rule, while the Australian and West Indies teams, mainly made up of Packer players, had). They insisted that we had a full evening for practice under the lights.

Many of these differences had still not been settled when we arrived. I suppose I put the English case firmly; at any rate I was regarded as its symbol, even its originator. This view was reinforced when, in our first night match against the West Indies at Sydney, I put all ten fielders, including the wicket-keeper, on the boundary for the last ball of the match. From then on, whenever I walked onto the ground, especially at Sydney or Melbourne, I was greeted by a tremendous roar of boos (not to mention booze).

Near the end of the tour, Bob Hawke, a leading trade union leader in Australia and a keen cricket follower, told me that he thought I could have mollified that hostility if only I had communicated in some direct way with the crowd. He didn't want me to leave the country with an entirely unfavourable view of his compatriots. They were his supporters, after all, and they were not bad fellows. I think he was right in saying that what annoyed them most was my apparent indifference, my ignoring them rather than, as Tony Greig would have done, responding with some gross and recognisable gesture. If I were to start that tour again with the benefit of this advice, I might make an attempt to share a joke with the crowd, but I could not communicate in this large-scale, flag-waving way. I am not Tony Greig.

Inwardly I coped with this onslaught better than I had expected, but the efforts at control, and the aggression that had to be harnessed for batting and strategy, took their toll. I felt very tired during the tour, and needed even more than before to get away from the cricketing environment whenever I could. It was, of course, my fourth consecutive winter playing Test cricket abroad. Most Test cricketers need the occasional break away from the game, a break of several months, to be really fresh.

On that tour, I batted better in Tests than I had done for a long time; but my captaincy deteriorated. George Mann told me that when he captained the MCC in South Africa in 1947–8 he never had dinner away from the hotel; he felt that he should be available there each night for the players. In 1979–80 I did not spend enough time with the team off the field. I did not know fully enough what their problems and feelings were.

It is of course much easier to motivate others when results are going well. In his book, *Put to the Test*, Geoff Boycott, writing about the previous tour when we won 5–1, considered that I 'did an excellent job on and off the field'. After the next tour he was more critical. Now, as he wrote in *Opening Up*, 'Mike's casual sort of captaincy encouraged a bad lack of discipline.' Further – 'the nets were often organised in a lackadaisical fashion. Ken Barrington, as assistant manager, was supposed to be in charge of net practices and he's a real expert at it. I'm not knocking Kenny, but he certainly didn't seem to exert the same influence as before (did somebody tell him not to?). He seemed to run the nets as a time-keeper rather than as a coach.' As one of the few in a position to 'tell him not to', I categorically deny any implication in these remarks that I tried to suppress Barrington or in any way diminish his role, nor do I know of any such attempt. But there is some substance to Boycott's criticisms. I did not have the energy to exert the necessary amount of discipline on that tour. I have always believed that self-discipline is preferable to discipline imposed from above and outside. England players ought to know best what practice they need. Moreover, not everyone derives as much benefit from incessant nets as Boycott does. When he took over from me in New Zealand I'm told that he had players travelling early in the morning before matches to distant grounds for net practice on hopelessly inadequate pitches. Such practice is of course counter-productive, as batsmen lose what confidence they have, and bowlers can only go through the motions. Nevertheless, there were times on the 1979–80 tour when I should have been more dictatorial.

Boycott's words also hint at a second line of criticism brought out more explicitly by another of my team-mates, Bob Willis, in his excellent *The Cricket Revolution*. Once again, the comments apply to this tour. Willis writes that I 'had my cricketing disagreements with Ken Barrington. Ken wanted to sort out the techniques of some of our young batsmen, an opinion I shared, but Mike would not allow it. He felt that if you are good enough to play for your country then you are able to sort yourself out.'

I am sorry if I gave Ken Barrington this impression. What I meant to convey was my caution about the value of coaching. Willis himself was my mentor in this attitude, for I have never forgotten his account of how his coach at Surrey tried to make him bowl with a classical action, left shoulder round: Bob literally could not bowl straight enough to avoid the side-netting! Far too many people want to turn others into pale imitations of themselves: Boycott did not help Alan Butcher before his first Test innings at the Oval in 1979 when he almost paralysed him with his account of the risks of playing shots in a Test match: the road to hell is paved with good intentions. During my dreadful loss of form in 1978 I had ten different pieces of advice from ten ex-Test cricketers in ten days. It is impossible for young players to with-stand such squalls of advice, and I am proud of having shielded – as I see it – Graham Dilley from some of it on that tour of Australia.

I tended, too, to defend a player like Gower from much of the criticism that came his way when he failed, for it seemed so often to be fundamentally inconsistent, if not dishonest. One day – when he played and missed 30 times – he would be lauded to the skies; the next, when he played better and got a touch, he would be berated for being casual and lazy.

However, perhaps my caution came across too strongly. Only once did I question Barrington's coaching, and that was for its timing rather than its content. On Brian Rose's first tour, in Lahore, Ken suggested that he should cock his wrists and open the face of the bat in pick-up. Excellent advice – but was this the right time for it? Such a change affects the whole of one's technique. Brian would have few enough chances on that tour, and a radical experiment was too risky. The three of us talked this out thoroughly. I was not aware that Ken felt any different about his role in 1979–80 than he had done on the other tours we went on together.

By the end of the 1979–80 tour I was ready for a rest. I had had enough, too, of the cricketer's life, of cricket conversation, the cricket environment, of the whole travelling cricket circus. Before I could embark on my training in psychoanalysis I had to commit myself to being in England all year round. I had put it off tour by tour for about three years, but now I was clear that the time had come to stay at home in the winters.

Surprisingly, I found myself looking forward to the county season. Reflecting on the tour, I decided to impose my will more emphatically, especially at the start. In March the Middlesex cricket sub-committee (who still had to appoint a captain for the season), concerned about our moderate results in 1979, asked what I proposed to do to rectify matters for 1980. They were conscious of my fatigue; and they wanted me to confirm that I was fully committed to the job. I told them that I intended to intervene more with advice and suggestions about the way players were tackling their game. I mentioned the problems of captaining a county side when I was away for half the season at Test matches, and pointed out that this was unlikely to happen in 1980. The committee were clearly satisfied, as they immediately recommended that I retain the captaincy. Perhaps this slight sting to my pride and the challenge to any possible complacency gave an additional charge to my motivation and concentration. Certainly when we returned in April I ran the nets myself and was demanding about practice and punctuality. I tried to imbue the team with a more ruthless attitude. We set out to win all four competitions.

I enjoyed my cricket in the summer of 1980 enormously. As it turned out, I was available for all of Middlesex's matches, so was no longer a sort of absentee landlord from early June onwards. One man – van der Bijl – made a huge impact on our side – not only on the field, where his figures speak for themselves, but also in the dressing-room. He saw the best in all of us and his fresh optimism gave many, including me, a boost. The humour in a side when each knows the others' weaknesses can well become biting, and Vintcent helped to counteract this tendency. We had a highly successful season – and, as John Arlott once said, while Test cricket makes money and establishes reputations, county cricket is more fun. We played on pleasant grounds, at Cheltenham and Scarborough, Worcester and Taunton, Uxbridge and Hove. I could go about my business with less sense of being peered at, scanned, taken to pieces. It is much easier at, say, Cheltenham to wander round the ground after getting out, buy ice-creams, and sit peacefully among the crowd.

In 1978 I had been awarded an OBE as England captain; an honour that made me feel I should be on my best behaviour in the future. In 1980, however, I was less inhibited, and allowed little bits of aggression to come out in my play. (Incidentally, Boycott, on hearing of my 'elevation', is alleged to have commented: 'If I'd gone to Cambridge I'd have got a Knighthood'.) During my best innings that year, when I scored 91 against Surrey on a fast, uneven pitch at the Oval, the crowd started to jeer me, so I marched towards them, shaking my fist and offering them the bat. I was quite good humoured about it; but I could no longer see why I should hide my reaction. There was another incident which attracted more attention than it deserved, when I had an argument with Imran Khan at a tense moment during the Benson and Hedges Quarter Final at Lord's. Imran complained to the umpire that Daniel was bowling too many bouncers. It was a bit rich, I thought, coming from Imran, so instead of keeping out of it I intervened and said, 'They weren't bouncers, they were below shoulder level. And, anyway, you tried to get it up but couldn't.' Imran got heated at this, but all would have quietened down amicably enough if Gatting, who must have been watching too many football matches, had not rushed over and pinioned my arms behind my back, giving spectators the idea that I was about to hit Imran. I wasn't – and not only because he was armed with helmet, bat and gloves. Gatting's charitable intervention earned him a flea in the ear, and me fantastically exaggerated reports in the papers. The *Daily Express*, for example, described it as the worst incident ever seen on a cricket pitch, and even *Wisden* wrote that, 'almost incredibly Brearley and Imran appeared on the point of grappling'.

At this point I should reassure the reader that I value the traditions of the game; I am appalled at the idea of even a verbal set-to between players. I don't recommend such behaviour, nor do I congratulate myself on it. However, there was a value to me in being a little freer in expressing my feelings, in unburdening myself of the weight of propriety that crowns the head of the national captain. ('That's not a crown,' Mike Smith once remarked to me. 'It's a coconut.')

Roland Butcher and I had some fruitful conversations in this area during that summer. He had noticed that every successful player in the Middlesex side had a full measure of his own style of, usually controlled, aggression. He admired the way Edmonds, for example, would often be stung into bowling at his best by the arrival of the opposition's best player, while Emburey would never allow his grip on a side to relax and would often pick up the last few wickets. Occasionally, too, Edmonds would snap his fingers at a lazy piece of fielding, and Emburey flush at the effort to contain himself when appeal after appeal was turned down. Butcher felt that only now was he allowing himself to accept and even to nurture his own aggression. He had been afraid, before, that people would hold any inadvertently aggressive remark against him; yet he liked the way Clive Radley and I, for example, showed in the slips a passionate desire to get rid of each batsman. Roland emerged more and more during the summer, both personally in his more robust interactions with the rest of the team and in his game, as a batsman and as a fielder. He ended the season with a best-ever batting average of 41.

A similar topic came up with Simon Hughes, our young fast bowler, who forced his way into the County XI by some fine performances in our Second XI. His ability was clear at once. But I felt that he almost compulsively needed to prove to himself and us that he was not yet capable of consistency as a fast bowler. As captain I found it frustrating that he should so often bowl casually at the beginning or end of an over. During our match against Essex, at the beginning of August, just after he had taken a crucial wicket, I tackled him with this. 'You bowl four beautiful balls on off-stump, perfect length and line, moving away; then you bowl two dreadful balls down the leg-side. Why?' He replied, looking down at his feet, that he didn't think he was good enough yet to bowl *six* balls an over right. There was a streak of illogicality and self-satisfaction in that remark which made me, momentarily, quite angry. I felt he was anxious not to set himself the highest standards, that he preferred, unconsciously, to be mediocre. I knew he had the highest talent, but he needed to be more ruthless, more unrelenting, more ambitious. Vehemently, I told him that of course he could bowl six balls an over as well as he bowled the four good ones.

Captaincy is, of course, an individual thing. There are as many styles as there are captains. I admire some captains who never lose their tempers or blame their own players unfairly. Ian Chappell once told me that he tried never to shout at players on the field. I'm afraid that I fail to live up to that standard. However, my overt impatience has one good feature. It shows that I *mind*, that my energy is flowing into the job. There have been times when this is not so, when it has seemed hard enough to motivate myself, let alone others. For most of 1980 I was thoroughly engaged as captain of Middlesex.

At the beginning of 1981, on the other hand, I felt unexpectedly sluggish. For the first time I arrived back a few days late for pre-season practice, and others, notably Daniel and Thomson (who had only recently signed), came back later still. Moreover, the four who had been to the West Indies arrived home after an arduous tour only on 17 April. So there was a ragged start to the pre-season practice. The poor weather in May hit us even worse than other counties, and our form was scarcely flattered by the fact that by mid-June we had won only one championship match. At about this time Butcher had asked me what my motivation was that year, and I had lightly replied 'to score thousands of runs'. That was all right, he said, but what of my ambitions for the team? I felt there was some truth in his implied criticism, and that my slight inertia might be echoed by the rest of the players. I called a team meeting. Butcher repeated his remarks, and Barlow supported them, adding that I had not been so firm or determined as the previous year. Downton generalised the discussion, saying that he had noticed a reluctance to help each other out at practice in the mornings. Out of that meeting came a renewed commitment to each other and the side.

As it happened, we gave our best performance of the season in our very next match, beating the eventual champions, Nottinghamshire, by 112 runs, and followed this with a streaky one-wicket win at Maidstone, where Knott batted brilliantly and Underwood took 6–29. Personally I had had a marvellous June, scoring four centuries. More to the point we had, at last, begun to play well as a side, and I felt I was back 'on song' as captain. I was, altogether, ready for the call.

There was also, throughout this period, another factor in my life sufficiently unusual to describe at some length, which helped my cricket and my captaincy. Without it, I doubt whether Bedser and his co-selectors would have had cause to come back to me. I started my psycho-analysis in September 1979, shortly before the start of the Australian tour. The tour itself created a 3½-month gap in the analysis, but since my return I had been going five times a week without interruption except for holidays. People sometimes refer to this process as 'undergoing' analysis, their tone of voice suggesting that it must be as enjoyable as surgery without anaesthetic. My experience has been different. I have actually enjoyed it. I find I am put in touch with parts of myself that in the rush of practical life I often ignore. In these sessions, I surprise myself by the range of imaginative thought of which I am occasionally capable.

Far from making me more 'analytic', more prone to stand back from my actions and feelings, the process has, for me, tended to encourage spontaneity. Of course one oscillates – between the flow of free association and the standing-back of self-observation – but the latter certainly has not worked like a dam. Some such oscillation is also required in captaincy. One tries to respond, like others in the team, to the situation and the players, but also to check that this natural response is not derived from one's own needs. To give an example: the captain who is an opening batsman should not allow his apprehensiveness about batting on a greenish pitch to affect his decision on whether to bat or field; but nor should he go to the other extreme to prove that he is *not* afraid.

Other oscillations are also called for. There are times when a captain must throw all his energy and con-centration into his own game, but he must never lose sight of the overall view. He must be warm and open with the players; but must be prepared to keep some distance, to avoid showing undue personal preferences off the field. He must be capable of firm autocratic decisions in a crisis; and of consulting his team whenever possible. He should intermingle optimism with realism. Psychoanalysis enables me to become aware of such varieties of attention.

There has been more direct assistance too. My analyst helped me in advance to imagine and deal with the aggression that was to be expected from post-Packer Australia – a sort of mental net. She hinted that their bravado might cover insecurities no less real than mine – a view partially confirmed later by Willis, who reported after a late-night colloquy with Lillee following the Birmingham Test in 1981 just how unconfident Dennis had felt all season, despite appearances to the contrary. Lillee's reputation and histrionics have sometimes, I'm afraid, increased his potency; at Perth in 1979 some England batsmen lost touch with their combative powers. In 1981, when Middlesex played the Australians, I was batting against Lillee with the new ball. He was still recovering from his illness and the pitch was easy-paced. I tried to 'work' a shortish ball to square-leg, turned my bat too early, and lobbed the ball into a large vacant area at mid-wicket. As I trotted through for a single, Lillee said sarcastically, 'Well played.' 'Well bowled yourself,' I retorted. Next day, when we passed behind the pavilion, Lillee said, 'Using a bit of psychology, eh, Mike? I didn't know what to say when you said "Well bowled."' A trivial interchange, perhaps, and a minimal challenge to the Great Man's ego, but without analysis I might have meekly ignored Lillee's remark.

I used to have a tendency to feel over-responsible for the failures of the team; my analyst helped me to remember the strengths of the side and the mutual responsibilities. I also came to appreciate the contribution a captain makes by protecting the players from much of the attention of the media by taking it on himself. I think, too, that my spontaneity and confidence as a batsman were helped by this process. In 1980, I scored more freely in one-day cricket than ever before, without losing my touch in three-day matches. Barlow said to me, jocularly, at Nottingham, that I should bring my 'shrink' along and see what she could do for him!

There are, of course, moments of gloom. And at times, in order not to miss sessions, I would go to analysis at 6.30 a.m., and travel to places like Southend, Basingstoke – or even, once, Nottingham – for the 11 o'clock start. I was so tired at Basingstoke that I fell asleep in the car park on arrival and was lucky to make it in time. I'm not sure, either, that Freud would have approved: in a paper written in 1914 he advocated making the patient 'promise not to take any important decisions affecting his life during the time of his treatment'. In the summer of 1981 it was not possible to take Freud's advice literally.

4

No More Skylarks

So much for the past. Practical questions raised by Alec Bedser's phone call soon crowded in. There was more than a week until the journey to Headingley, a week in which Middlesex had, unfortunately, only one day's cricket.

I started to consider what line to take with the media, and wondered about the composition of the side. I thought that I should try out my new bat, and ask Duncan Fearnley, who makes mine, for a spare. I was keen to talk at once with one of the England players, to gain a sense of the team's attitude to Ian's resignation.

The question was, which player should I contact? I should have liked to talk with Ian himself, to sympathise with him and to wish him well, but I refrained from trying to reach him – partly because I thought he would like to be left alone, partly because I wanted to be sure that the selectors shared my view that he should play in the next Test. (I later discovered, incidentally, that one current player felt that we were wrong to pick him as, in his opinion, Botham needed a break from the tensions of Test cricket altogether.) Willis, too, might not have been a certainty for Leeds in everyone's book, so I was reluctant to seduce him into a false sense of security. I should have liked to talk to my Middlesex colleagues, Emburey and Gatting, but had heard that they would be travelling to Nottingham; they had taken the chance to play in a three-day game against Sri Lanka rather than go so many days between Tests without match practice. Other players, too, would be travelling, and in some cases I did not have a telephone number to contact them.

Graham Gooch is a keen observer of cricket and cricketers; he seemed certain of selection, and lives in London. So I rang Graham. His view was that the current side probably comprised the best players in England but that they had not yet played *at* their best. He said that they had gradually fallen out of the habit of practising close-catching; and that team talks before sessions of play had become rare. He felt that at Lord's on the second day the side should have been reminded of the need to keep going, to pile up a huge score. It is, on the face of it, curious that Test players should need such pep-talks. In fact, at any level of cricket they can be useful. They cut through the air of enjoyable relaxation brought about by lunch or tea; they remind everyone of targets or of basic cricketing truths; and, above all, they can help morale. At Hendrick's instigation at Sydney in 1978–9 we started to have intense, brief meetings before every session; these talks helped to revitalise a unit that had become sloppy and dispirited. The philosopher R. C. Collingwood has written that 'a tribe which dances a war-dance before going out to fight its neighbours is working up its war-like emotions.' We do not go as far as the New Zealand rugby teams with their Maori dances; but pre-Test dinners and pre-session talks have in part a similar purpose.

Gooch's remarks made sense. I also felt, strongly, that one major problem for the team must be the blunt fact that they had played 12 consecutive Tests without a win. A sequence such as this means inevitably that the expectation of success fades. Such expectation makes a big and infectious difference. The bowler is more likely to induce a catch if he and the slip-fielders are confident that they will hold it, and they in turn will catch it if they think it will be induced.

Alec had told me that the announcement of my appointment would be made at 9.30 a.m. the next morning, 8 July. The simplest way of dealing with requests from the media for interviews was to ask Lord's to arrange a press conference, which I did for mid-day. I also decided, perhaps over-conscientiously, to have a net on the same visit.

I had been having trouble with my bats. One had broken, and another sounded twangy, as if there were some deep crack. Fearnley had recently sent me a new one (but only after some nagging from me). Also the batting gloves he had had specially made for me in India during the winter had been lost in transit, and the replacements had only just arrived. So I decided to try them out together with the new bat. Like many current players, I have grown over the years from a light to a much heavier bat. When I started, my bat weighed about 2lb 2oz. Five years ago, I used one weighing 2lb 5oz. Two years ago it was 2lb 7oz, and now my best bats were around 2lb 10oz. This new one felt a bit heavy. I found I had to push more with my right hand, and was not playing as straight as I had throughout June. This net, in front of some twenty photographers, did not help my confidence, though it was good to have Don Wilson, the MCC coach, bowl left arm over the wicket as Bright had done during the Lord's Test. When I got back to the dressing-room, I weighed the new bat. 2lb 15oz! No wonder I couldn't swing it properly. One advantage of my reinstatement was that Duncan had two more bats, of the right weight, at Paddington Station for me on Friday morning.

The press conference went off well. I was wary over questions about the likely side as there were still two days before the selection meeting. It seemed plain, though I did not explicitly say so, that Woolmer would have to make way for me; and I did say that my initial reaction was to keep Boycott and Gooch together as openers. I said, truthfully, that I was not closely in touch with the form of Test contenders or with the trends of selectorial thought. For this Test I should depend more than usually on the opinions and knowledge of the other selectors. Officially, the captain is only one among five, not *primus inter pares*: if it comes to a vote, his view carries no more weight than anyone else's. However, in practice the selectors are unwilling to stand in the way of a captain when he is determined on a particular choice. In my opinion, this is as it should be, for the captain needs to have as much confidence as possible in the players under him, as he, after all, has most to answer for when things go wrong. However, in my experience it was rare that I was convinced of a certain view in opposition to all or most of the others.

I was also asked about Botham and me: would there be any problem in having the deposed captain in the side? I was confident that there would be none. I reminded them of how helpful Tony Greig had been in 1977. I knew Ian well, we got on, and it was a bonus for me to know that he had said he hoped I would be the one to replace him.

With hindsight, the greatest irony of the events leading up to the match lies in the fact that Bob Willis, who bowled us to the fantastic win on the last day, so nearly was not picked at all. At Lord's, suffering from a debilitating chest infection, he had bowled 32 no-balls. After the match, he went straight home to bed.

On Friday at 5 p.m. the selectors met as usual in a small room on the third floor of the pavilion at Lord's. The routine had not changed; I enjoyed being back with Bedser, Charles Elliott, Brian Close, and now John Edrich, eating salad and cheese and drinking beer and wine in the small back room upstairs on the Friday evening before a Test. One familiar face was, of course, not there: Ken Barrington's. I missed his warm twinkle, his concern, his seriousness suddenly melting into a chuckle. How he would have relished the outcome of the series, and how anxious he would have been through most of it!

Willis' fitness was the first topic when the meeting began – a few minutes late, as Close had just hurried down from Yorkshire. Alec told us that he had spoken to

Bernard Thomas earlier in the day. Thomas had said that Willis should be fit for the Test, but that he would not be playing for Warwickshire over the weekend 'as a precaution', and that he would rest until Tuesday, when he would have his first work-out. We were not happy with this. Bob had had recurrent 'flu-like infections before, and had been severely weakened by them. His illness at Sydney in the 1978–9 tour had initiated a period in which for two and a half Tests he could not find his old rhythm or speed. Moreover, in the last two series in which he had played Bob had faded after a good start; his body seemed unable to keep going through the ardours of a full season. Before he left for the West Indies in January, I had suggested to him that he should not start playing until shortly before the Tests, for fear of blowing himself out too soon. As it happened his knee collapsed and he came home before the Tests began. Alec tried to phone Willis during our discussion, but could not find him. However, he did talk to Thomas again, who said that Willis could probably start training on Monday rather than Tuesday. Even so, we were afraid that it would be too risky to play a fast bowler who was no longer young, who had this history of illness and its after-effects, and who would have had only a couple of nets before this crucial five-day Test. We felt that it would be in his own best interests, and ours, if he missed Headingley and made sure that he was fully fit for Birmingham. We left him out; but Alec was to explain the situation to him as soon as possible.

Three front-line bowlers were chosen without much debate: Botham, Dilley and Emburey. We all felt that Ian should have at least a couple of Tests free from the captaincy. He had not been bowling with his old zest, but he had looked better recently. Anyway, he was irreplaceable. Dilley had a remarkable striking-rate in Test cricket, and in the two Tests this summer he had taken twelve wickets in only 69 overs. He often took a wicket in his first over or two. Despite being erratic, he was, we thought, our main strike bowler. The selectors were disappointed that Emburey had not taken more wickets when bowling into the rough at Lord's. There was some talk of including Underwood, for whom the rough outside the left-handers' off stump would be even more helpful, but we were all convinced that Emburey was our first spinner and likely to contribute with the bat and in the field. We could not see ourselves picking two spinners for Headingley (though at that time we certainly expected to play one!).

We talked at some length about Chris Old and Hendrick. Old had been bowling at his best. As captain of Yorkshire, he was turning in far longer spells than before. He tends to pitch the ball up further than Hendrick, so that he has more chance of bowling batsmen or getting them LBW. He has always enjoyed bowling at left-handers, and Australia had four in their top seven. As I had not seen Hendrick so far, it was hard for me to have a firm view; but I was happy to have Old on his home ground at Leeds, where in May he had taken six for 100 in 48 overs against Middlesex.

The remaining places were quickly filled, though Knott was mentioned (and pencilled in as reserve). As cover for Emburey we talked about Eddie Hemmings – a much improved off-spinner who was having a fine season for Notts – as well as Underwood. Our batting reserve was Wayne Larkins, who had played well against Sri Lanka. We all agreed not to disturb the Boycott/Gooch opening combination. Gower, Gatting and Willey would all be happier to stay where they were at 4, 5 and 6. I had already reconciled myself to going in at No. 3. John Cleese suggested that I memorise the last twelve scores – 10, 5, 0, 0, 2, 1, 3, 1, 0, 0, 21, 9 – made by England's No. 3, and rattle them off at press conferences in case of difficulty. John and I also joked about Lillee's frequent exits from the field to change his shirt; he was indeed both delicate and valuable to Australia, and we envisaged a Pythonesque extension of his special treatment in which he was borne down to fine-leg on a bejewelled palanquin after every over.

Fortunately the side that we had chosen did not remain unchanged. Alec contacted Bob next morning at the Oval, where Warwickshire had just started their Championship match against Surrey. Bob was, I think, flabbergasted at the news. He would, he said, have played in the county match if he had known we would want him to. He still had a slight cough, but otherwise was already fit. Unfortunately, Warwickshire had by now announced their side and started the match, so he could not play. I had conversations with Willis, Bedser and Thomas when I came home around tea-time. I told Bob that in my opinion he should play on Sunday and again, for the Second XI, on Tuesday. In between, on Monday, he should bowl at least twelve overs in the nets, flat out. Then, by Wednesday, we would know for certain whether he could last through a Test.

The team had not yet been announced or revealed to anyone, so the chairman was able, by phoning the other selectors, to gain agreement that Bob be put back in the twelve. Even so, he still nearly did not play.

My father drove me to Leeds on the Wednesday morning. He was anxious lest the VW that I had sold him five years before broke down. We drove off the motor-way near Nottingham and had a chilly picnic in a field. I walked alone some 200 yards along a track to the middle of the field where the only sound was a skylark in full-throated ease. From now on, I thought, no more picnics and skylarks! Rather the clangour of battle, the uniforms of conflict. I had taken my England cap and sweaters out of the drawer where I had expected them to lie, awaiting the moth. I had shaken the creases out of my England blazer with its lions on the pocket (the same blazer which had once in a shop in Cheapside provoked the question 'What do them kittens stand for?'). I had also drawn my allocation of the new football-style team shirts. They are made of a clinging material, more suitable for muscle-rippling torsos than for my kind of physique. Besides, there's so little room inside for a chest-protector that I had to borrow one of Botham's extra-large shirts at Leeds! Hughes, Border and Botham combine with these shirts white track-suit bottoms for batting; all of which is very different from the billowy flannel shirts and generous creams of recent years.

We reached Leeds without alarms by 2 p.m., an hour before the team was due to gather at Headingley, which is a suburb about two miles from the centre of town. I dropped my suitcase off at our hotel, and went to the ground. Superstitiously, I took a different peg from the ones I had used before, and changed near the door, next to Bob Taylor (who was to be 40 on Friday). A few of the players were there already: Peter Willey, who manages to be sardonic and warm at the same time, a true professional who lets no one get away with any nonsense. Willis was there too. He told me he was fit. Eleven overs, nought for 17, against Leicester Second XI the day before, he said, grinning – *and* they'd lost! Boycott came in soon, grumpy: they had put the television in his corner. With bangs and mutterings ('twenty years in this seat' etc) he shifted the TV, while Willey raised an eyebrow and the corner of a lip. 'Both' came in and cheerily turfed Mike Gatting out of the seat he, Ian, had occupied for all his four Tests at Leeds since the first in 1977 when we won back the Ashes against Greg Chappell's side. Any uneasiness that he might have felt was concealed beneath his jokes and vitality.

When I got the chance, an hour later, of a quiet word with him I commiserated with the way he had been pursued. I said he would probably score a century and take twelve wickets in the match – which would make up for it. 'You're in a Catch-22 position,' I joked. 'Do well, and you're not a captain. Do badly and you can't even play!' He laughed feelingly, in full agreement. More seriously, I also told him that he must get into the habit of playing straight while having a look at the ball; he had too often been LBW or bowled playing straight balls to square-leg. He had already taken Edrich into a net with him to throw balls at him just for that purpose: to get into the habit of playing them straight back.

Thomas and I talked of fines for being late, a pound a minute, instituted by Botham. I had heard that the system had fallen into disuse; and I was, anyway, against the idea. But Bernard talked me round, saying that fines had helped to make one or two more punctual on tour (especially Butcher and Gower, apparently), and the money did go to a charity. At the end of the season we were able to give £200 to the Muscular Dystrophy Society.

I was glad to have Thomas there, to take care of the exercises, and Edrich, to organise the nets. I had asked John to help me in this way and to talk to the players if he noticed anything wrong with their techniques. During the match I had an interesting conversation with him and Close about the weight of the bats used by current players. They convinced me that it is easier to adjust against the moving ball with a lighter bat. The heavy one may be best in the West Indies, say, for strong players like Gooch and Botham. After this – and after trying to bat against Lillee and Alderman on the Headingley pitch – I asked Fearnley to send me a lighter bat.

The Headingley pitch! We looked at it, felt it, pressed it, stamped on it for many minutes that afternoon and early the next morning, trying to extract its secrets. Despite its whitish colour and the clear surface cracks running both across the pitch and up and down it, it was not dry all through. Keith Boyce, the groundsman, told me that he had discovered that there were no drains under the square. Although the pitch itself had not been watered for sixteen days there would still be moisture underneath. Boycott pointed to the coarseness of the grass. The 1977 pitch, on which he had scored 191, was different, with fine, consistent, greenish grass; not so thick in its blades or, presumably, so strong in its roots.

We did not think that the cracks would crumble or really 'go' but they would accentuate variation in bounce, which helps quick bowlers more dramatically than slow. Top-class seam-bowlers would always be hard to play, especially if – as the forecasters predicted would happen at least until Saturday – the weather stayed overcast.

Certainly batting in the nets gave no batsman the illusion of an easy match. Emburey and Willey, turning it in one net, were still a relief after Dilley and Willis in the next. In the third net, we could play a few shots against some youngsters and one valiant grey-haired seam-bowler (who came every morning of the match and would bowl as long as we wished). Facing Dilley, I was struck by the change in his bowling. Instead of swinging the ball in, he curved it sharply out. Moreover, the ball seemed to come from a different place – lower and wider than before. He bowled few balls I had to play at.

After my knock in the nets, and some slip-catching practice, I did the usual pre-match interviews. Those with television and radio were routine enough, though I did have the opportunity to say how unattractive I found the new electronic scoreboard. At that time I did not realise that its drawbacks were not merely aesthetic; we later discovered that its surface reflected a bright sky so that the numbers were hard to read from the playing area.

I had no idea that an 'issue' was awaiting me at the press conference. The subject was Lillee and his shirts. I knew of course that Lillee had been ill, but I had felt slight concern about the regularity and length of his absences from the field after each spell of bowling, and I voiced this concern informally in the course of a private conversation with Donald Carr, secretary of the TCCB, that took place on the day of my appointment as captain. I wanted to know what the laws of cricket stated on the subject, and whether there had been a special agreement between the teams. Carr showed me that according to the rules a player was entitled to a substitute only if he was off the field because of illness or injury; Botham had not objected, but the Board shared my anxiety. Carr had himself already decided to take up the matter with Fred Bennett, the Australian manager, and was pleased that I had mentioned it.

I had thought no more about the subject until the following weekend when I was shown a copy of the *Sunday Express*, in which I was alleged to have 'written a letter of complaint' about Lillee's behaviour. I was puzzled by the provenance of the story and irritated by the distortion. Now, at Leeds, I was at once confronted by a series of aggressive questions on the topic, and was asked to react to Hughes's comments. It appeared that the Australians felt that I had made a complaint behind their backs (whereas I simply had not yet seen them since being made captain). Hughes had added that it was a slur against the great fast bowler to imply that he was doing anything other than change his shirt, a precaution needed after his recent bout of pneumonia.

Feeling attacked by the tone of the questions, I'm afraid that I retaliated with a more vehement and clear-cut view than I actually held. Instead of underplaying the divergence and simply saying that I would discuss the matter with Hughes before the match, I described a future in which a team of specialist fielders relieved bowlers and batsmen of this chore; I suggested that if we really wanted such a game we should have it by negotiated agreement and not by default.

Dealing with the media is like being a cat on a high wall, picking one's way between the pitfalls of unnecessary concealment and indiscretion. My punchy – and inappropriate – response suited the popular press well, and next morning the story was prominently displayed under the headline (in one paper) TEST WAR. Untypically, I think, I had fallen into a trap. First, a writer had come to hear of a confidential remark. This had then been exaggerated and presented to the 'affronted' party (Hughes), whose heated defence had then been put to me. Thus a 'row' had been created out of virtually nothing.

At last, I managed to leave the ground. I decided to have a bath at the hotel, and returned, as Colin Cowdrey was wont to do, in whites, to prepare for our pre-Test dinner and team talk. I had already had some useful conversation with key players. Willis confirmed that Both's decline in form meant that it was hard to know whether he should be regarded as a strike bowler or as a stock bowler. He was not now swinging the ball sharply. Although his form had improved recently, it was well short of his Bombay level. Bob said that Dilley ('Picca' to us) needed mothering; he has to be encouraged, unlike Ian, who responds well to being called an old fart. 'Picca' should bowl in short spells after an initial longer one. The possible waywardness of both these two meant that Emburey should be used more in a defensive role on goodish wickets. (At this stage we were not thinking in terms of four seamers; that idea grew gradually as we reflected on the parallels with Trent Bridge, as well as on our uncertainties about Botham and Dilley.) Bob added that he rated Gower and Gatting, who seemed in good form, as slip-fielders.

We gathered at 6.30 p.m. and sat round the dining table. The selectors would join us for dinner at 7.15 p.m. Boycott started by commenting that we could beat Australia primarily if our bowling and fielding returned to its old standard; he had noticed that we were not so lively when we failed to take a wicket for some time. We reminded ourselves of Sydney in 1978–9, and of Nottingham in 1977, when we sent Australia plummeting from 101–1 to 155–8 on an excellent pitch. 'They only have two top-class batsmen,' Geoff said, 'Hughes and Border.' 'And Wood?' I asked. 'Maybe,' he replied. Willis said, generally, and in particular about Wood, 'Let's have a third man; let's stop them scoring so fast.' Gatting had spotted that Border goes a long way back early in his innings, so maybe the quicker bowlers should pitch the ball further up to him – not half volleys, but fuller than usual. Boycott added, looking at Botham, 'And our medium-pacers shouldn't bowl too many short ones at him.' Yallop was different. At the Middlesex team talk before we played the Australians, Thomson had told us that Yallop was always extremely nervous when he first went in, and Emburey confirmed, from his contacts with the Victorian players, that all the State sides bowl their quicker bowlers at him. Certainly he had been too high in the order so far, going in at No. 3. Thomson had also told us that he often had Hughes LBW; and I stressed how important it was for anyone who could force him on to the back foot to do so. We should not, though, bowl many bouncers at Hughes unless the conditions favoured us, as they often got his run-rate, and his adrenalin, going. We remarked on Dyson's skill at leaving the new ball; we stressed the importance of making him play. I remembered a ploy that Lillee used against me in the second innings of the Centenary Test when I left a lot of his deliveries; he bowled some slower inswingers which were less likely to bounce over the top than his full-paced balls; two of them narrowly missed the off-stump when I let them go. Dyson also tended to lunge at the medium-pacers, so we might need a short square-leg and silly mid-off. We did not spend long on Chappell, except to say that he was mainly an on-side player; we should keep the ball on or outside his off-stump.

Marsh would be No. 7. People felt that he was less dangerous than in the past, being particularly prone to being caught LBW if the ball moved in to him (as at Lord's and Trent Bridge). We remembered his straight drives, hits to leg and, on the off, his square-cuts. We asked the bowlers not to be too friendly to Lillee and Lawson; both are useful batsmen, especially if the ball is pitched up. Willis said, 'And don't be afraid of having a deep mid-wicket; they're both liable to hoik it over there.' Bright was recognised to be a useful nightwatchman.

Hogg and Alderman were not, as batsmen, lingered over.

We did not spend much time on the Australian bowlers. I asked about Alderman, whom I had not faced in England. Willey said, 'He's quicker than he looks; he hits the bat hard.' They all had a healthy respect for him. Willis said of Lawson, 'He's quick for six overs, isn't he? But then?' Hughes tended to bowl his quicks in very long spells, and Lawson could not keep up his top pace for long. We knew Lillee well enough. Botham said, 'You can forget about Dennis being quick; he's not well, he's medium-paced.' He may have been by the time Botham faced him; with the new ball he could still be quite sharp, as we were to see at Headingley. We also knew Hogg: nowadays he was more patchy as a performer, more unpredictable than when he bowled so marvellously in 1978–9; there were still, as we knew, doubts about his fitness. Most people were so convinced that they would play four seamers, as at Nottingham, that there was not, as I remember, much discussion about Bright's bowling.

I asked the players what they felt about Lillee and his shirts. Their opinion was that we should not make an issue of it. 'He thrives on the adrenalin-charge of a row,' said Boycott. 'Remember the aluminium bat at Perth?' They thought that whether he was off for five minutes or ten made little difference. The main problem was practical – what could we do, and how would strong action affect *us*? If I happened to be batting when Lillee finished a spell, would I be able to concentrate fully if I took the controversial step of refusing to allow a substitute fielder? And could I ask other batsmen to take that stand? A better solution would be to gain agreement with Hughes that no bowler on either side would take advantage of the opposition's leniency by remaining off the field for longer than was necessary. The umpires too could be asked to keep an eye on excessive absences. I had never in ten years' captaincy refused a substitute while a bowler changed his shirt; it would be foolish to start now.

Routine matters were also dealt with during the evening. Alec handed round our car-park tickets and the complimentary tickets (four per day per player) and the special lunch and tea tickets (two per day). The begging and bartering of tickets began. It is rare that there are any spare tickets until, perhaps, the fourth or fifth day; any that are left over are usually given to Bernard Thomas who acts as a sort of agent to whom those with late requests can apply. We also settled the important question of time of arrival at the ground.

There was some confusion about hours of play. The traditional hours (11.30 a.m.–6.30 p.m.) had been provisionally changed to 11 a.m.–6 p.m. at a time when it was hoped that the Australians would agree to the experiment of requiring a minimum of 100 overs per day. Even an 11 a.m. start might have been too late if the finish had been put back an hour because of bad weather, and if on top of this there were ten or fifteen overs to be made up. When Australia declined the experiment, it seemed sensible to revert to orthodox hours – except at Trent Bridge where all the tickets had been issued with the earlier hours, and at the Oval where the shortening days required an 11 o'clock start. However, Yorkshire too had issued tickets which advertised an 11 o'clock start, and they thought it unfair on the public to announce a further change. So, oddly, we ended up starting three Tests (the first, third and sixth) at 11 a.m. and three at 11.30 a.m. To add to the confusion, the first, fourth and fifth had play on Sundays (from 12 to 7 p.m.) while the others had the traditional Sunday rest day. At our dinner, there was some minor grumbling about the variability of hours (at Lord's, apparently, Kim Hughes had come to toss up at 10.35 a.m. thinking the start was 11 a.m.). The important point was to work back from the start by – we agreed – 40 minutes. At that point everyone would do some fielding practice and especially the eight who might find themselves in the slips. (Only Willis and Boycott did not fit into this category.) For Thomas's exercises we fixed on a time ten minutes before this, i.e. 10.10. These exercises would not be compulsory, but it would be nice if everyone took part together especially on the first day. As for nets, they were a matter for individual choice; I stressed that nets should not clash with the ten minutes put aside for fielding. Many players do not like to be on the ground for too long before a Test, as the tension builds up too early. So I merely said that the latest time I wanted anyone to turn up was 9.45.

Over dinner, I continued my conversation with Boycott. In reply to my question about whether he was conscious of any decline in his batting, he said, 'No, I don't think so. Certainly I'm a better player at forty than I was in my twenties. And look at the bowlers we've played against during the last couple of years!' I felt the same, about him and about myself. He was encouraging about my batting; 'I wish I'd scored four centuries this season,' he said. He felt the rest from Test cricket should help me; he reckoned that those who had been to the West Indies might be jaded; and thought it significant that of the two who had played best so far this summer (Gatting and Gower), one had not played much on the tour, and the other had taken a complete holiday before the start of the English season. I asked him about his views on the balance of our side and on whether to bat or field if we won the toss. He reckoned we should put off batting as long as we could, as he knew the ball would bounce awkwardly; and, if the cloud stayed, it would seam. Boycott added that he normally preferred a balanced side, but would be tempted to rely on Willey, now fit to bowl. And Tests are almost never won at Leeds by spinners. Botham and Gooch, on the other hand, reckoned that the dry crust on the pitch would allow spin from early on. Old was convinced that the seamers would be helped more than the spinners. I went to bed totally uncertain on this crucial issue. I slept well, better than four years before, when I had my futile late-night foray into the zen techniques of Japanese archery, and proceeded to get out to the second ball of the Test match next morning, caught by Marsh off the bowling of Thomson.

Next morning I had breakfast at 7.30 a.m. with Willis and Elliott, and went early to the ground with Bob in his bill-board of a station-wagon. I knew that I wanted the reliable Old, plus Botham as all-rounder, and Dilley as a strike-bowler. For me, the choice lay between Willis himself and Emburey. Bob, who probably imagined that Old would be left out if Emburey played, opted – uncertainly – for four seamers. Finally, I too came down, with equal tentativeness, on the same side. The selectors inclined the other way, but let me have the side I preferred.

Hughes and I went out to toss at 10.40, when the clouds lifted a little. He announced, to my surprise, that Hogg was the one to be left out of their twelve. He called heads, and won.

It was mid-July, but felt like mid-April. Hughes asked the umpires what was the latest time he could decide. He came in to the pavilion and took Marsh and Lillee to have a second look at the pitch. In our dressing-room, Boycott donned his elbow-guard and chest-protector, Gooch his two thigh-pads, the second one on the inside of his right thigh. The bowlers, too, were tense, warming up. At 10.50 a.m. Kim told me that Australia would bat.

At last the umpires went out. A moment later, I felt that peculiar *frisson* down my back as I stepped on to the Headingley ground as captain of England once again.

5

The Headingley Test

After the first day's play, I almost wished I had not come back. Australia were 210 for 3; that was bad enough on a strip about which I said to umpire David Evans shortly before the close, 'If all went well, you could bowl a side out for 90 on this pitch.' Worse was the thought that – before the match had even begun – I had been responsible for a glaring error: we left out Emburey. In mid-afternoon, I had brought Willey on for a few overs. He is not in Emburey's class as a spinner and still had a bruised index finger, which necessitated his using his second finger to spin the ball, yet he had made several balls turn and bounce – on only the first day! Emburey would not only have been able to attack; he would also, on the day's evidence, have been more accurate than all our seamers apart from Old. Before tea, when Boycott and I found ourselves at extra-cover and mid-off to Willey, I said to him (not without a tinge of reproach, I fear) that the pitch was already helping the spinner. He, more level-headed, retorted, 'This pitch helps all sorts.'

After play, Marsh did not help matters by asking, on his visit to our dressing-room, if our omission of Emburey had been a bluff to get them to put us in to bat. I suppose that it was some sort of tribute to our cricketing sense that our selection had caused Hughes to take Marsh and Lillee for the second look at the pitch, to reinforce their decision to bat first.

Back at the hotel, I could not sleep for a long time, brooding over the choice. I thought, 'They've not brought me back for my batting; and now, before the Test's even started, I've made a tactical howler.'

16–21 July

AUSTRALIA First Innings

J. Dyson, b Dilley	102
G. M. Wood, lbw, b Botham	34
T. M. Chappell, c Taylor, b Willey	27
K. J. Hughes, c and b Botham	89
R. J. Bright, b Dilley	7
G. N. Yallop, c Taylor, b Botham	58
A. R. Border, lbw, b Botham	8
R. W. Marsh, b Botham	28
G. F. Lawson, c Taylor, b Botham	13
D. K. Lillee, not out	3
Extras (b 4, lb 13, w 3, nb 12)	32
TOTAL (9 wkts dec)	401

T. M. Alderman did not bat.

Fall of Wickets: 1–55, 2–149, 3–196, 4–220, 5–332, 6–354, 7–357, 8–396, 9–401.

Bowling: Willis, 30–8–72–0; Old, 43–14–91–0; Dilley, 27–4–78–2; Botham, 38.2–11–95–6; Willey, 13–2–31–1; Boycott, 3–2–2–0.

Second Innings

J. Dyson, c Taylor, b Willis	34
G. M. Wood, c Taylor, b Botham	10
T. M. Chappell, c Taylor, b Willis	8
K. J. Hughes, c Botham, b Willis	0
G. N. Yallop, c Gatting, b Willis	0
A. R. Border, b Old	0
R. W. Marsh, c Dilley, b Willis	4
R. J. Bright, b Willis	19
G. F. Lawson, c Taylor, b Willis	1
D. K. Lillee, c Gatting, b Willis	17
T. M. Alderman, not out	0
Extras (lb 3, w 1, nb 14)	18
TOTAL	111

Fall of Wickets: 1–13, 2–56, 3–58, 4–58, 5–65, 6–68, 7–74, 8–75, 9–110, 10–111.

Bowling: Botham, 7–3–14–1; Dilley, 2–0–11–0; Willis, 15.1–3–43–8; Old, 9–1–21–1; Willey, 3–1–4–0.

ENGLAND   First Innings

G. A. Gooch, lbw, b Alderman	2
G. Boycott, b Lawson	12
J. M. Brearley, c Marsh, b Alderman	10
D. I. Gower, c Marsh, b Lawson	24
M. W. Gatting, lbw, b Lillee	15
P. Willey, b Lawson	8
I. T. Botham, c Marsh, b Lillee	50
R. W. Taylor, c Marsh, b Lillee	5
G. R. Dilley, c and b Lillee	13
C. M. Old, c Border, b Alderman	0
R. G. D. Willis, not out	1
Extras (b 6, lb 11, w 6, nb 11)	34
TOTAL	174

Fall of Wickets: 1–12, 2–40, 3–42, 4–84, 5–87, 6–112, 7–148, 8–166, 9–167, 10–174.

Bowling: Lillee, 18.5–7–49–4; Alderman, 19–4–59–3; Lawson, 13–3–32–3.

England followed on.

Second Innings

G. A. Gooch, c Alderman, b Lillee	0
G. Boycott, lbw, b Alderman	46
J. M. Brearley, c Alderman, b Lillee	14
D. I. Gower, c Border, b Alderman	9
M. W. Gatting, lbw, b Alderman	1
P. Willey, c Dyson, b Lillee	33
I. T. Botham, not out	149
R. W. Taylor, c Bright, b Alderman	1
G. R. Dilley, b Alderman	58
C. M. Old, b Lawson	29
R. G. D. Willis, c Border, b Alderman	2
Extras (b 5, lb 3, w 3, nb 5)	16
TOTAL	358

Fall of Wickets: 1–0, 2–18, 3–37, 4–41, 5–105, 6–133, 7–135, 8–252, 9–319, 10–358.

Bowling: Lillee, 25–6–94–3; Alderman, 35.3–135–6; Lawson, 23–4–96–1; Bright, 4–0–15–0.

England won by 18 runs.

Umpires: B. J. Meyer and D. G. Evans.

Next day I told Emburey I was sorry; we had been wrong to leave him out and the decision had been mine. John tried to reassure me, though I knew he was disappointed and guessed he was critical. By the end of Saturday's play, however, after I had seen the Australian pace trio operate, the initial selection seemed more defensible. In fact, on Sunday I phoned Emburey to hear about Middlesex's week-end, but also to tell him that I was not so sure now that I had been wrong. Ironically, there were times not only on Monday but even on Saturday when Hughes would have been delighted to have a fourth seamer rather than his spinner. If we had had to start another Test a week later on the same pitch it is possible that Australia would have picked Hogg and we Emburey. Who would then have been bluffing whom?

The first day's play was indeed frustrating. We had no luck, and missed some chances. Only Old bowled consistently well. For Australia, Dyson played with sense and grit to score a maiden Test century.

The day started with a cool breeze blowing from backward square-leg, opposite the pavilion. Willis and Dilley both preferred to come up the hill from the Main Stand End, with the wind slightly behind them. Old and Botham wanted the other end. Such an amicable division is rare; and as the match went on, the wind veered in front of square so that later on all four were keen to bowl from the Kirkstall Lane End. At times a captain has to point out to his bowlers that someone has to bowl the other end, and that batsmen cannot choose theirs; but hills and winds do make a difference to them. Running downhill, a bowler is liable to bowl no-balls, over-pitch, and generally lose control; I was glad that Willis and Dilley chose the other end since they are both prone to no-ball. On the other hand a bowler who runs in up the hill may find himself under-pitching, and, especially if the wind too is against him, lose his fire.

I started with Willis and Old, Old because he usually

makes the batsman play at every ball, Willis because I thought he would not waste the new ball as Dilley might. The innings began as it was to continue. There were some loose balls, put away for fours over the fast outfield; and the good ones beat the edge of the bat. I remember one over from Willis in which Wood thick-edged him between third slip and gully to the boundary, then eased a wide half-volley the other side of gully, also for four. We had started with a leg-slip for Wood; Botham had noticed how far over Wood gets, with the result that he can edge it fine on the leg-side. Moreover, he sometimes 'picks the ball up' to long-leg. But the area behind square on the leg-side is large for one close-catcher; besides, we needed more cover on the off-side, so leg-slip had to go. Against Dyson, I soon had two short-legs for Willis, who was bringing the ball back awkwardly into his ribs. Dyson edged both bowlers streakily past the leg stump; then a lifter from Willis hit him near the wrist to be taken by Gatting at short-leg. We appealed: not out. Gatting told me later that he was convinced the ball had hit the batsman's glove, but such decisions are often impossible for the umpire: most of us were uncertain, anyway.

Dilley replaced Willis, and over-pitched. Dyson drove him straight for four, and Wood hit a full-toss past cover. Old's opening spell was excellent. Normally, he likes to have a mid-off, so that he is more confident about pitching the ball up. Though the ball was not swinging much, it was bouncing awkwardly and sometimes moving off the seam, so I moved from mid-off to an attacking position. First I went to slip, then to silly mid-off, in case Dyson, who tends to lunge forward, popped one up off pad and bat. Alternatively he might be 'conned' into playing back more often, which would suit Old. Remarkably, Chris did not take a wicket. Replacing him, Botham, with his third ball, which was little more than a loosener, had Wood LBW. 55–1.

Trevor Chappell came in at No. 3, and stayed with Dyson for more than 2½ hours. This was a crucial stand that put Australia into a strong position. Chappell did the job that he was selected for, protecting the better players at four, five and six from the new-ish ball and from the bowlers at their freshest. To our chagrin, we helped him on his way. First Gower missed a hard chance off Botham at third slip, when Chappell was three. Not long after, Botham missed a much easier one off Willis. Next over Botham, who had moved to gully to have a break from slip-fielding while he was bowling, missed a hard catch as Dyson slashed at a short ball from Dilley. Poor Ian! His early success with the ball seemed a long way back; he had hurt his arm while making a fine pick-up and throw; and now the crowd began to get at him.

Both Chappell's chances had come when he was brought forward; when the ball was short of a length he was ruggedly in line. And now we gave Dyson opportunities to score off the back foot. I had known him to be a useful player off his legs; the forcing off-side shots that he played in this innings were a revelation to me. The batsmen became more audacious in their running between the wickets, which was annoying, though Gower, now at cover, nearly ran each of them out. Old continued to bowl well, and for a few overs Willey troubled both batsmen, without being accurate enough to keep close fielders in and thus the pressure on. The batsmen were looking well on top when Willey had a stroke of luck, Chappell edging a near long-hop outside the off-stump to Taylor.

Play was extended to seven o'clock as more than one hour had been lost through showers. The day ended in sunshine, with Dyson cruising to his century, and Hughes quietly playing himself in. We were looking to the new ball which would become available early the next morning. With 40 minutes to go, I bowled Boycott for three overs – not, as Marsh wryly suggested, to curry favour with the Yorkshire crowd, but because he would swing it in the strong breeze, and might make Hughes over-ambitious. As a last fling I gave Dilley the ball at twenty to seven; he would have time for two or three overs down the hill (and, now, with the wind); out of the blue he at once yorked Dyson. This late wicket at least enabled us to look forward to the morning with some optimism. Their score at close of play was 210–3.

The next day, Australia consolidated their position without ever dominating. However, I thought Hughes was right when he said after play '400 was worth about 1,000 on this pitch.' The press were carping about the day's play, Woodcock saying that it contained 'little of the quality, or the cut-and-thrust expected when England meet Australia.' I thought, on the contrary, that Botham, Willis and Old bowled well, while Hughes and Yallop played with much determination. And in the last two overs of the day, after Australia had declared at 401 for 9, Alderman bowled a ball to Gooch that went past his 'chin-end' (as they say in Yorkshire) from a good length, while the so-called medium-paced Lillee made Boycott play five balls down from almost shoulder-height.

For England, the best feature of Friday's cricket was Botham's bowling. On Thursday, I had seen from close quarters what I had suspected from a distance, that he was running in more slowly than he had eighteen months before. Moreover, I noticed that just before reaching the crease he stepped in towards the stumps, which reduced his momentum. The purpose of this manoeuvre was to swing the ball more by getting his left shoulder further round. But the outcome was the gentle swing that Willis had warned me about. At his best, he comes in like a bull charging, with an action that is straightforward, uncomplicated and unfussy. I encouraged him to come in straight, to *bounce* in, as lively as he could. It was at Headingley, I think, that I started to ridicule the jink in his run-up, calling him the 'Sidestep Queen'.

On the second morning I gave the new ball to Old (up the hill this time) and Dilley. The latter had a nightmare spell, in which he could not bowl straight, though when he did he first hit Bright in the box and then next ball bowled him. The crowd, with their baleful, derisive 'Bowl at t'stumps', upset Graham, and he gestured expansively when he took the wicket. After four overs of Dilley, I brought Ian on, with a rather caustic comment, I think, about not just floating the ball up like a middle-aged swing-bowler. He retorted (with reference to the previous evening, when I took him off after only three overs) that he would take five wickets if I gave him a decent spell. 'How can I bowl in three-over spells?' he added. For the rest of the day, I can only remember one time when I thought of taking him off, though I did keep checking that he felt fit to continue. The weather was a little warmer than on Thursday, so perhaps the ball swung more easily. At any rate, the elaboration designed to achieve movement was scrapped. His old rhythm and sharpness gradually returned, and he fully deserved his figures of six for 95.

Willis, too, bowled better, though utterly without luck. He gave Hughes, in particular, a torrid time. Both Hughes and Yallop fought admirably, putting on 112 runs. For most of this time we still had three or four slips and a gully, all of us expecting to be in business at any time. Another two slip catches went down. Gooch dropped a straightforward one from Hughes off Botham when Hughes had scored 66; and I just got a hand to a low, wide chance from Yallop off Old. Hughes played some characteristic shots: a racy pull high over mid-on that reminded me of his 99 at Perth in 1979, and a couple of electrifying cover-drives. Yallop cut well, and played some nice straight drives. I was criticised for not bowling Willey for more than two overs in the course of the day: but I would do the same again, as the quick bowlers looked likely to take wickets every over.

At last a wicket did fall – Hughes tried to push Botham wide of mid-on, turned his bat too soon as the ball swung away and lobbed the ball back off the leading edge. He was out for 89. Two more wickets followed soon afterwards. Then Marsh briefly showed the power of his straight drives. He and Lawson had an easy time until Botham, belatedly in my opinion, bowled a bouncer which Lawson fended off desperately to give Taylor an easy catch.

The declaration came as a relief to us all, except our openers. It is odd that we do not seriously contemplate night-watchmen for opening batsmen. I suppose they (I should say 'we') are happier going out to face the music at the start. As Boycott once said, 'I'm used to going out with someone else and coming back by mi'sen'. Taylor was lined up to go in if a wicket did fall. As usual, I would not countenance having two night-watchmen since, if both were used, Botham would be batting at number nine.

It had been a long two days. I was out of the habit of fielding for twelve hours. In the morning Bernard's exercises had loosened me, but I had felt less nimble than the day before. Willis had already looked stiff by Thursday evening. Now after two days Dilley was discouraged. I had a talk with him in the shower (the provision of washing facilities at Headingley is niggardly, only one shower and two baths to be shared between the home side and the umpires.) Graham bemoaned the fact that so many people had talked him into changing his action and trying to bowl closer to the stumps. He said that Holding had noticed in the West Indies that he was not bowling *naturally*. I said 'Look at the number of top bowlers who are really quick, bowl from wide of the crease, and swing the ball *in*: Croft, Procter, Daniel, Willis and Garner, for a start.' I wondered if he could go back to his old ways. He said no, that would only make things worse. I could only remind him of his fine Test record and his potential as England's fastest and most promising bowler.

I was called upon all too soon on the Saturday morning, Gooch playing across Alderman's first ball. It swung down the line of the middle and leg stumps and caught him LBW. I narrowly escaped a similar fate against the same bowler without scoring, and was grateful for an inside edge to square leg to get off the mark. I was struck by the silence of the crowd, as Lillee came in. Moments of greatest tension are often marked by the most hushed quiet. Once or twice an over the ball behaved alarmingly. One ball to Boycott shot straight along the ground, just missing his off-stump; the next, from the same length, reared up and hit him on the gloves. I was full of admiration for Geoff's skill; he hardly played and missed at all. I also admired the new gloves that he had designed and made for himself, with small strips of fibre glass protecting each section of finger. I had already benefited by modelling my own gloves on an earlier version of his; the foam rubber protection on the outside of the index and second fingers of the bottom hand is taken right round the end of the finger. In addition, extra finger-stalls, like the ones used in wicket-keeping gloves, prevent serious injury to these vulnerable finger-ends. With his latest design, Boycott felt no pain. What is more, he seems to have done away with the occupational hazard of cracked or bruised fingers that can make it impossible to play at one's best, if at all.

Both of us tried to 'graft' our way through. We aimed to let the ball go outside the off-stump, and scored only by nudges or deflections. We hoped to wear down the bowlers. Fortunately, Lillee did not bowl at his best. His line was not what it used to be. I remember facing him in the Centenary Test at Melbourne, where, bowling with six slips, a square cover, short-leg and deep fine-leg, he never strayed to the leg-side of middle stump and never bowled wide enough of the off-stump to be left without risk. At Headingley, he bowled several balls quite wide on either side. Having bowled them he would chide himself; 'Come on, Dennis. What *is* that, Dennis?'

As usual, there was no 'sledging', just occasional exclamations of frustration. Lillee and Alderman are, nowadays, somewhat similar in their style. Both swing their stock ball away, but can bowl an inswinger. Both cause the batsman trouble when he looks for an outswinger but the ball comes straight or perhaps moves marginally in off the pitch. Neither is afraid of the batsmen driving them. At Headingley they were desperately difficult to play. After an hour I edged Alderman to Marsh, and five minutes later Boycott was bowled by Lawson, who had replaced Lillee. Boycott's dismissal illustrated the vagaries of the pitch. Lawson bowled a ball from wide of the crease, pitching just short of a length, well outside off-stump. Boycott went over behind the ball: he would normally be looking to play such a delivery down from waist height. Instead the ball cut back *and* kept low, taking his leg-stump. It was an impossible ball to play.

Gower, as often, lent his touch of class to the proceedings with some easy drives, especially off Alderman. But he too was out to an unplayable ball, immediately after being missed by Dyson in the slips. Lawson bowled the next more quickly, on a good length; Gower pushed forward but the ball leaped viciously to touch his glove, and Marsh took the catch above his head. Gatting too had been dropped in the slips, by Wood off Lillee, but did not last long.

So when Botham strode out to join Willey the score was 87 for 5. He had commented before he left the dressing-room that he did not intend to hang about, and he immediately played with abandon. Early on, he tried to smash a ball on the off-side and missed; he looked up to the balcony where I was sitting. I grinned and indicated that he should have tried to hit it even harder. He smiled hugely. He played some magnificent shots, especially on the off-side, reaching 50 off only 54 balls. At once, he set himself to force Lillee through the off-side, then tried to get his bat out of the way as the ball reared sharply, touching his glove on the way. He thus became Marsh's 264th Test victim. Brian Close, sitting beside me on the balcony, reckoned that Ian lost concentration after making 50. I didn't agree. If you set yourself to attack on such a pitch and the ball behaved oddly you had to be lucky to miss it. Yet only by his commitment to attack had Botham been able to change – for a while – the complexion of the game.

In most circumstances I have felt that each batsman at Test level should figure out the method of play that gives him the best chance of success, and in the conditions at Headingley this guideline – or lack of one – was particularly apt. For me, the option was to struggle along as best I could, inevitably on the defensive for most of the time. For Botham, on the other hand, with his wonderful eye and strength, playing his buccaneering shots was the best bet. But whatever method anyone used, he would require a fair share of luck to survive.

Botham's dismissal was a landmark in the history not merely of this particular game but also of cricket. Marsh thereby passed Alan Knott's record of dismissals in Test cricket. This he achieved in 71 Tests against Knott's 93. Of the 264 victims only 11 were stumped, compared with 19 for Knott. These figures reflect the extent to which seam bowling has predominated in modern cricket, and, too, the transformation in the nature of the cricket played when the few spinners that are left carry out their work. Bert Oldfield, between the wars, stumped 52 out of a total of 130 victims. Rod Marsh is, of course, a superb 'keeper, wonderfully agile for a man of his bulk. He is, typically, short; has there been, at least in the last ten years, a top-class keeper as tall as, say 5' 9"? Off the field, he is quite different from what his public manner might suggest; quiet-spoken, humorous, the first to congratulate opponents when they do well. On the field, he embodies the uncompromising, trenchant aggression of the best Australian sides. However, he plays the game with total honesty. When a ring of Australian slip fielders appeal resoundingly for a catch or an LBW, Marsh may well be the one who remains silent. (Though when he knows a batsman has nicked it but has not been given out, he has not always kept that conviction to himself!) Finally, like many great performers, he has humility about the game, and enjoys learning more. At the end of the 1979–80 season, he told me that despite having scored few runs he had learned a great deal about batting that year, and clearly relished the fact.

Back to Headingley. We were all out for 174 at tea on Saturday. We were not surprised when Hughes invited us to follow-on. Had Sunday not been a rest-day, his decision could have been harder; the situation would have been more like the one confronting Illingworth at Adelaide in 1972 when his main bowlers were exhausted. On the whole, my view is that as captain you may hesitate before enforcing a follow-on; but you do it.

There was short delay because of bad light. On resumption Gooch, facing Lillee, was at once beautifully caught at third slip. This was a perfect delivery, just outside off-stump, moving away late. As soon as I reached the middle the umpires offered us the chance to go off. Decisions about light are among the hardest for umpires, but it is particularly galling to the batting side when play is suspended immediately after a wicket falls. We were held up for just over an hour. I remember thinking how everything was falling into place for Australia. The weather was warmer again when they bowled, which helped them to move the ball. Botham had begun to punish the three tiring pace bowlers, but they dismissed him and the tail-enders before becoming too exhausted. Now they pick up a wicket in murky light, and then have an hour to rest up before attacking again.

However, big black clouds still loomed, and we had to face only three more overs, which included two high, fast leg-cutters from Lillee and a half-volley which I gratefully drove for four. Because once again more than an hour's play was lost, close of play was rescheduled for 7 o'clock. The rule stated, however, that conditions had to be fit at 6 for this to happen. At 5.55 the umpires inspected; one black cloud still held us up. At 6 play was called off for the day, but five minutes later bright sunshine was filling the ground for virtually the first time. Spectators jeered and threw cushions in disgust. It was unlucky that the very rule brought in to give the public value for money should have caused such dissatisfaction – and ironical that these fiascoes should have occurred on two consecutive Tests. In my view the rule was illogical; once the time for the close of play has been put back, this later time should act like any other end-point of play.

I was certain that we would lose, unless it rained for at least a day. At the press conference after play I said that in my opinion we had not batted badly. 174 was about par on this pitch, and we would have made even less if Lillee had been at his best. I sympathised with the groundsman who, like Allsop at Trent Bridge, had paid the penalty of not playing safe, of not settling for a moribund and dreary wicket. (I had asked Gatting earlier which of the two was the more difficult to bat on. He thought Headingley was, as the odd ball kept even lower here; which meant that one could not leave the shortish ball just outside off-stump for fear that it would not only break back but also fail to bounce above stump height.) I added, finally, that my experience of writing at Trent Bridge and of playing in this game confirmed me in my view that those in the press-box had the easier job!

On Sunday, I went to lunch with a friend near Harrogate, where the British press were due to play the Australian press at cricket. Christopher Martin-Jenkins wanted an experimental match played on a 22 metre pitch (which sounds attractive to batsmen facing constant fast bowling, but would in fact equally hamper the spin bowlers), but no-one else did. It rained much of the afternoon but the English press won a shortened game on a pitch of normal length. I told my host that if our game lasted till the Tuesday – which I doubted – I could let him have a ticket.

The last two days of the Headingley Test were the most extraordinary and unbelievable that most of us have

witnessed. Just after three o'clock on the fourth day our
score was 135 for 7. We were still 92 runs behind. I did not
feel unduly depressed. The outcome had seemed almost
inevitable from, say, Saturday lunchtime. The batsmen
had not disgraced themselves. For once, an England
defeat would be attributable more to the bowlers and
fielders than to the batsmen. Besides, my mood is often
lifted by a conversation with Rodney Hogg. During
the Monday afternoon, we sat on the balcony, and he
amused me with his account of his game on Saturday for
Ramsbottom in the Lancashire League. He had had no
problems with his back, but was pleased, mainly, to have
scored some runs. His bowling had gone well too until
some 'cowboy' had slogged him all round the field. He
was not so impressed, either, with his lift home. He was
dropped in the centre of Bradford, seven miles from his
hotel. I was interested in Hogg's experience of the
League: my overriding memory of him at his best, under
Yallop's captaincy, is of his unmitigated distaste for any
spell longer than four overs, and I knew that the star
bowler in the Lancashire league is expected to bowl the
entire afternoon. In fact, Rodney went on to discuss Kim
Hughes's handling of the quick bowlers. Did I think
that Kim kept his bowlers on too long? We discussed
Lawson's prodigious effort at Lord's, and Alderman's
everywhere. I recalled Willis's early Test experiences
under Illingworth, when he was used solely as a shock
bowler. On the other hand I had at times bowled Botham
for extremely long spells, as I did in this match. I said, 'It
looks as though you'll get away with it here.' But as we
talked the miracle was beginning. Botham and Dilley
were laying into the tiring Alderman, Lillee and Lawson.
As the carnage increased, Hogg thought he'd better go
back to their dressing-room to rejoin the other non-
players, and I went into ours, to share the enjoyment of
our ascendancy while it lasted.

The best batting before this partnership had come from
Boycott and Willey. I had fallen exactly as Gooch had; I

could not play that ball in any other way. It might, I think, have dismissed even Boycott, though his technique – bat held so loose – means that if he edges the ball it does not carry so far. Gower was subdued; unable to score for half an hour, he took nine runs in an over from Lillee before edging Alderman to slip. Gatting was LBW yet again. Sometimes he plants his leg too early and too far over so that his bat cannot come straight down to the line of the ball. At 41 for 4 Willey joined Boycott, and in totally different styles they played very well. Willey struck six fours on the off-side: anything pitched up he drove firmly, and the shorter balls he smashed anywhere in the arc between extra-cover and third man. For Lillee, Hughes took Dyson from the slips and put him at squarish third man, two thirds of the way back. As Willey shaped to cut, the ball moved in to him, cramping him for room to play the shot. Instead of lambasting the ball square, he was only able to slice it to Dyson: such immediate rewards for intelligent and inventive captaincy are rare. Boycott batted for 3½ hours, and played even better than on Saturday. He was beginning to play some off-side shots – I particularly remember an extra-cover drive off Alderman – when, surprisingly, he was LBW with his front foot half forward. So Dilley joined Botham.

I started to think of the formalities at the end of the game. One drawback of captaincy in Tests is that at the very moment when, after five days of battle, one most wants to subside with players of both sides, the captains have to go on public view. First, there are the interviews on two television channels immediately after the match, followed by various radio stations. Then we meet the press. The whole operation can take an hour, and by the time it is over the dressing room is half empty and littered with glasses, beer cans and debris. I decided to pack my bag now and change, so that at least I would not come back to find my gear strewn over a wide area and half the side gone. I showered and changed. However, feeling that a striped shirt might be seen as too blatant an admission of defeat, I changed back into a cricket shirt. Gooch told me later that he too thought of changing and noticed that I had done so; but he thought better of it for himself.

Botham was not the only one to have booked out of the hotel that morning. I would have done so too, except that since Middlesex were due to play at Old Trafford on Wednesday, I would be staying in the north. It was a pleasure for him to book back into the hotel on Monday night, and for me to unpack my bag again for the 10.30 start on Tuesday. So, how did it happen?

Botham started relatively quietly, scoring 39 in 87 minutes before tea. He said afterwards, tongue in cheek, that he was playing for a not out! It was Dilley who at first played more aggressively. His method was to plant his front foot somewhere near middle stump, and swing the bat hard at anything to the off-side of where he stood. He hit – and missed – very hard. After tea, Ian hit even harder. I remember some outrageous strokes, a wind-up aimed at mid-wicket that sent the ball way over the slips, and another that went off the inside edge behind square-leg for four. (He was using Graham Gooch's bat, who claims the patent for the off-drive that the Fearnley inside edge speeds away to square-leg. 'He hadn't used it much during the match,' said Ian later, 'and I thought there were a few runs left in it.') Overall, Ian played wonderfully. He was particularly severe on Alderman, who was kept on until he was exhausted. Botham drove him over mid-off, through extra-cover, past gully. He went down the pitch and hit him splendidly straight for six.

In the dressing-room, we started to think of making Australia bat again – this target, 227, we reached while Dilley was still in – and of lasting out until the next day. It might easily rain on Tuesday, after all. Gradually, our hopes became more ambitious. If Dilley could stay with Botham until the close . . . At a quarter to five, however, he was out for 56, playing on to Alderman who was by

IAN BOTHAM'S 149 NOT OUT AT HEADINGLEY

KIRKSTALL LANE END

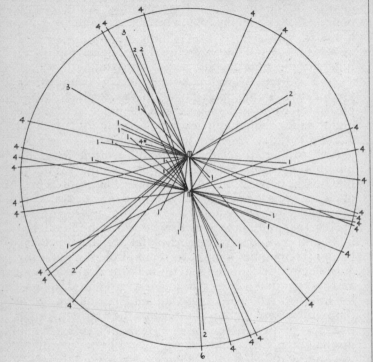

MAIN STAND END

Runs	Balls	Minutes	6s	4s
50	57	110	-	8
100	87	155	1	19
149	148	219	1	27

Bowler	Balls	Runs	6s	4s
ALDERMAN	62	68	1	11
BRIGHT	21	15	-	3
LAWSON	44	44	-	8
LILLEE	21	22	-	5

BOTHAM'S SCORING SEQUENCE

0002042000040100001000410000031
0013014204*0010000404000004040400
444104000000640100040 4†400010201
0001000100010040001000401042041 00
401000441000400000000.

* 4 overthrows to the mid-wicket boundary
† off a no-ball

© BILL FRINDALL 1981

Bill Frindall's run chart of Ian Botham's hundred.
Notice the number of runs made through or over the slips.

then bowling round the wicket to give the batsman less room for his shots. This was his first Test fifty; the stand was worth 117 in 80 minutes. Since tea, the pair had added 76 in 44 minutes.

Despite this exhilarating stand we were in effect only 25 for 8; our elation was, realistically, for two magnificent individual innings. Willis said, fiercely, to me, 'Make Chillie *play*!' We sent Old on his way with a mixture of pleas, exhortations and threats, the latter largely from Willey. Chris is a talented striker of the ball, but one of those batsmen whose initial movement against quick bowlers is back towards square-leg. However strenuously he orders that left foot to stay its ground, it always rebels. On the television screen, inside the pavilion, Willey wedged a bat handle against Old's bottom, trying to keep it in place. Chillie did his best, and so did his back foot. Together they accompanied Botham as he reached his hundred – off only 87 balls – and added 67 runs against an increasingly desperate side reduced by this fierce onslaught from magnificence to mediocrity. The desperation was highlighted by two beamers in an over from Lawson to Botham, after which umpire Evans spoke to Hughes. The beamer has been universally condemned by cricketers as an unfair delivery since the best batsmen have been unable to pick it up even in bright sunshine when well set.

What could Australia have done? I know well the feeling of impotence that Botham can engender; we have felt it often enough at the hands of Richards. However, I did feel the Australian seamers went on too long bowling their orthodox line just outside off-stump. Admittedly, Botham, Dilley and Old were all liable, even at times likely, to be caught off the outside edge. But they were often hitting the ball hard, or missing altogether; and the edges cleared the rapidly diminishing number of slips. And despite my reluctance to bowl Willey I was surprised that Bright did not come on at all until the score reached 309–8. I should have wanted to try him much sooner, though with a defensive field. When he did bowl, he came within a hair's breadth of hitting Botham's off stump.

The dismissal of Old was not the end, either, for Botham protected Willis so well that he had to face only 5 balls in the last 20 minutes, and we added another 31 crucial runs. At the close we were 351–9, 124 runs ahead. Another 60 or 70 runs, we felt, and we would actually be favourites!

Afterwards, I made the mistake of going into the Australian dressing-room. I had been there on Saturday evening, when they were cock-a-hoop. Perhaps I went too soon, for in the few seconds that I stood there I sensed thunderous silence, like the moment of Doom, everyone frozen in postures of dejection. Not even Hogg responded to my arrival. At last someone, I think Peter Philpott, the team coach, asked me if I was looking for anyone in particular. I went out again. Certainly the last thing I wanted to do was crow or appear to gloat.

Ian was keen to avoid the reporters. He asked me to tell them that he didn't want to talk. We escorted him through the crowds with a towel gagging his mouth. One newspaper made the best of a bad job with the caption 'Actions speak louder than words'. Half a dozen of us went to Bryan's Fish and Chip restaurant up the road from the ground. We got a round of applause – a rare thing, I imagine, for the friendly but staid clientele of this splendid eating-house. Like a group of John the Baptists we were preparing a path for one greater than ourselves – for Ian and his family came in soon after. Poor Liam Botham, probably overwhelmed and excited by his long stay at the cricket, got a bone stuck in his throat, and his day ended in tears.

Back at the hotel we had a provisional celebration. I offered to buy Ian a glass of his favourite brandy. First I gave him a measure of their worst cooking brandy and asked him to guess its age. 'Twenty years', he said. The Hine Antique turned out to be orange liqueur, but he did recognise that. I remember asking Graham Gooch where he would, ideally, choose to bat in a Test match. He said that he must have the best chance of personal success at No. 4, but obviously was happy enough to bat in any position. We also talked to Goose. He suggested that in the first innings we had been too concerned to bowl a good length and let the pitch 'do' the rest; should we, and he in particular, bowl faster and straighter? I agreed. 'Zap' underlined the point; 'Even Gatt's harder to bat against when he really runs in,' he said. 'And you'd better forget about no balls', I added. They too had made him tentative. On a pitch with such uneven bounce the harder the ball hits it the more devastating the variations will be. Moreover, bowling tomorrow would be an all or nothing affair, a huge effort without thought of conservation of energy.

We were due to start at 10.30. This time we all booked out. We exercised at 9.40, and commented regretfully on the weather. It was a warm sunny day, better for batting. At 9.50 we had some catching practice. I had decided to go back to first slip myself. In the first innings I left Gooch there, mainly because I was not fully confident having recently dropped two or three slip catches for Middlesex. What worried me most was not that I had dropped them, but that on one occasion I just did not react at all. By now Botham must have been feeling utterly confident and relaxed; I would keep him at third slip, and have Gooch at second from which he would not have to move when Botham bowled. Graham was quite happy to move away from first slip as he had had only two chances there in 2½ Tests and had dropped both. We would keep Gatting at short-leg, the position he had taken over from Woolmer. Willey was the specialist gully, and Gower could go back to the position he excels in, cover-point. I was glad to settle on this pattern. I like to captain from first slip; the players become accustomed to looking for me there, and I can see how the bowler runs in and what the ball is doing. The chopping and changing of slip fielders that had gone on in the first innings and in the other Tests is undesirable; it reminded me of Yallop's problems in 1978–9. Slip fielders need to be comfortable with each other, to learn each other's habits.

Willis had a brief batting net. We have given up attempts to coach him, and now leave him to his idiosyncratic ways.

Hughes took the new ball at once, and put all the fielders except for two slips back for Botham, who declined singles. The field came in for the last two balls, and Botham was unlucky not to strike a four or two. We had scored only five more runs when Willis was out. Botham was left not out on 149. It was one of the greatest innings ever played, even though it was to be surpassed only two Tests later.

I said a few words to everyone. 'More aggression, more adrenalin, more encouragement for the bowlers. The Australians will be nervous now'. I also told the four seam bowlers which of them would be starting. Clive Lloyd always gives the new ball to the same pair out of his four quick bowlers. I found it harder to decide. Botham still owed us six wickets, as I reminded him. After all that had happened since Friday morning, I thought that he was most likely to create another miracle so I gave him the new ball. His first ball was a long-hop, the second a swinging half-volley: Wood hit both for fours to leg – hardly a propitious start. At the other end, I went for Dilley. His batting, too, should have lent him confidence. I also thought that if the match became tense it would be impossible to bring him on for a first spell when we had few runs to play with. I would give him two or three overs in which to click; if he didn't, I would bring Willis on early.

In the third over of the innings we had a stroke of luck. Wood drove at a full half-volley, edged, and was caught by Taylor. I appealed only half-heartedly, wondering if the ball bounced after hitting the bat. TV replays showed the umpire to be right. 13–1. Botham had his first wicket, but Dilley was still struggling, it seemed. In two overs he was hit for 11 runs, without bowling badly. He would have to come off. He was, moreover, feeling a strain in his thigh. I sent him to have Bernard Thomas look at it; he was back on the field within a few minutes with the message that he could bowl through the injury if needed.

For the sixth over, I gave the ball to Willis. He said to me, 'Faster and straighter, right?' I nodded. At once he bowled well, up the hill. Botham wanted the other end to help swing the ball; but in the bright sunshine it was swinging little. Chappell and Dyson struggled on, beaten from time to time, but still there. We kept a third man and square-leg to stop the edges going for too many runs. After he had bowled five overs, Willis said to me, 'Give me a go at the other end.' Still thinking of Old's possible outswing from that end, my reaction was, 'You mean you've had enough of coming up hill into the wind?' This acknowledged Bob's problem, without committing myself. He said, grumpily, 'Okay, I'll carry on here then.' I put the question to Taylor and Botham during Old's next over. They both thought I should give Willis the end he wanted. Ian said, 'He's looked our most dangerous bowler.' I agreed. We would give Willis his head. To switch them, and to see how the pitch would respond to spin, I tried Willey at the bottom end. I still thought we might miss Emburey's ability to put pressure on the batsmen with close fielders on each side. After three overs of Willey I went back to Old who, like Willis, bowled with more aggression than earlier in the match. In fact, his contribution as the accurate, mean foil to Willis proved invaluable. Until Bright took 10 off his last over, he was hit for only 11 runs in 8 overs.

Meanwhile Bob was steaming in downhill. At last his – and our – luck changed. The change coincided with the return of the clouds, though no amount of cloud cover could explain the reversal that followed. First Willis bowled a perfect bouncer at Chappell, not too short and dead straight. Chappell, protecting his face, could only lob the ball up for Taylor. Next over, Old twice hit Dyson painful blows on the hand as he pushed tentatively forward. There was nothing tentative about the bowling or the fielding now. Willis summoned up all his energy for his last over before lunch. The first ball, not too short but lifting, just outside off-stump, was to Hughes. It may have straightened marginally off the pitch – Bob's natural inswing action sometimes causes the ball to move off the seam towards the slips. Up on tip toe, Hughes was not quite over to the ball, or over it, and edged it low to Botham's left at third slip, where the 'old' Botham took a fine catch.

The score was 58–3. Len Hutton once said that in 1954–5 he first thought they had a chance when Neil Harvey, playing for New South Wales against MCC, had to take his pad off to rub his leg after being hit by a ball from Frank Tyson. 'It must have hurt,' Len said, musingly. I first thought we had a real chance at Headingley when Hughes was out for nought. A few minutes before, Taylor, Gooch, Botham and I were talking about the frustrating near-misses of the past 14 months, twice at Nottingham, and then at Lord's when the loss of four hours for bad light had been crucial. We agreed, being realistic, that, as at Trent Bridge, Australia would probably scramble home by four or five wickets. (I don't, incidentally, believe that predictions like this imply defeatism or loss of aggression.) There was now less than five minutes to lunch. We roused Bob still further; he must fancy getting Yallop this time. 'Short and straight', we said. Three balls later Yallop had gone, beautifully caught at short square-leg from a nasty, kicking delivery. 58–4. We lunched – most of us in the dressing-room at such a crucial stage – knowing that the odds must be down from 500–1 to 6–4.

We spent some time guessing how the remaining Australians would play. Marsh might well 'have a go'; in the first innings at Nottingham he had slogged a quick 19 before being caught off a skier at long leg. Dyson, Border and Bright would 'graft'. Lawson and Lillee, if we got down to them, might have a swing, especially if we pitched the ball up. One thing was clear: we must keep running at them, harrying their batsmen.

Old struck next, just 13 minutes after lunch, knocking Border's leg stump out of the ground. 65–5. Next over Willis dismissed Dyson. In the previous over the Australian opener had hooked Bob easily for four. Now he tried the same stroke to another bouncer and, a little unluckily, gloved the ball. He was through the shot too soon. 68–6. Two overs later, Marsh too tried to hook Willis, top-edged, and Dilley judged the awkward catch perfectly, taking it a few feet inside the boundary. 74–7. Between overs, Bob came up to me to tell me that umpire Evans had told him not to bowl bouncers at Lawson, the new batsman. I was amazed. 'Forget it,' I said. 'But don't bother with an out-and-out bouncer at first – short of a length, rib-height.' Next over, with his first ball to Lawson, he put an end to all debate, having him caught behind for a single. 75–8. Willis had taken six wickets in six overs; Old had taken the other. In 58 minutes seven wickets had fallen for 19 runs on a pitch playing little worse than in the first innings, when, against the same bowlers, the same batsmen had amassed 401 runs.

The extraordinary match still had an unnerving twist or two in its tail. Australia may have been 75 for 8; but they still needed only 55 to win. In four overs, Lillee and Bright scored 35 of them. When Willis dropped short, Lillee stepped back and half-cut, half-poked the ball way over first slip for four (a shot he must have learned from bowling at Knott). At once I put a man back in that direction. Again Lillee found room to cut, this time beating Dilley at wider third-man. When Willis bowled more to leg, Lillee flicked him uppishly but safely behind square on the leg-side for three, then cut him for another four. Bright weighed in with two solid blows over midwicket off Old, and suddenly we were back on the defensive, on the brink of defeat. Gatting made a good point. 'It doesn't matter too much what length Goose bowls to Dennis,' he said, 'provided that it's straight.' Sure enough, Willis bowled a straight half-volley and Gatting himself took his second excellent catch, as Lillee, trying to play more conventionally, contrived to spoon the ball towards mid-on. Gatting took a second to judge how far the ball was coming, then raced in, dived, and caught it just off the ground. 110–9. I took Old off, and brought Botham back. We gave Bright a single. I asked Ian if he wanted a third slip or a gully. 'Third slip,' he said. Agonisingly, two sharp chances went to Old in exactly that position. Perhaps it was as well that the recipient was a Yorkshireman. The crowd would have been less patient had it been Keith Fletcher. It did cross my mind at that time that a Test could go down in history under the name of the man who dropped a crucial catch. Remember Fred Tate's Test in 1902!

A few moments later it was all over. Appropriately, Willis finished it with the perfect, most emphatic ball – a middle stump yorker which bowled Bright. Australia were all out for 'Nelson' – 111. It was the second time in Test history that a side had won after following on. Bob Willis had come back from the borders of oblivion to set the Ashes alight.

My Harrogate friend cut work for the first time in 20 years, and arrived at the ground when Australia were 56 for 1. He told me that he had never before left a cricket ground hoarse.

Soon after the close I received a telegram from Doug Insole which read, simply: ILLOGICAL STOP CLOUSEAU.

6

Lightning Strikes Twice

Another cable awaited me at Lord's when I returned to London, from Spike Milligan, which read: MARVELLOUS HAVE MY TICKET FOR THE WEDDING. I never found out whether this generous offer was in earnest. I knew that on the day in question, when Prince Charles and Lady Diana Spencer were to be married in St Pauls Cathedral, we would be travelling to Edgbaston for our next encounter with Australia.

And what an encounter it turned out to be! Less than two weeks after the amazing climax at Leeds the Australians found themselves in a similar last innings nightmare. This time the target was 151, 21 runs more than at Headingley, but on a better pitch, with an outfield if anything even faster, and in perfect sunny weather. It was a situation almost any Test team would dream of. But for Kim Hughes's side the memory of the disaster of Leeds was raw. It *could* all happen again; they must have faced the prospect of their second innings with superstitious foreboding, while we were fired with conviction by the recent miracle. After two days of the match, when Australia had a slight advantage, Kim said to me at Bernard Thomas's garden party, 'I only hope we don't have 130 to get again.' Unlike Brer Rabbit, he really didn't want to find himself in that particular briar-patch.

From beginning to end, the match was the most heated, combative and occasionally petty of the series. The balance of the game swung first one way, then the other, Australia having the better of it for most of the

Fourth Test, Edgbaston, 30 July–3 August

ENGLAND First Innings

G. Boycott, c Marsh, b Alderman	13
J. M. Brearley, c Border, b Lillee	48
D. I. Gower, c Hogg, b Alderman	0
G. A. Gooch, c Marsh, b Bright	21
M. W. Gatting, c Alderman, b Lillee	21
P. Willey, b Bright	16
I. T. Botham, b Alderman	26
J. E. Emburey, b Hogg	3
R. W. Taylor, b Alderman	0
C. M. Old, not out	11
R. G. D. Willis, c Marsh, b Alderman	13
Extras (b 1, lb 5, w 1, nb 10)	17
TOTAL	**189**

Fall of Wickets: 1–29, 2–29, 3–60, 4–101, 5–126, 6–145, 7–161, 8–161, 9–165, 10–189.

Bowling: Lillee, 18–4–61–2; Alderman, 23.1–8–42–5; Hogg, 16–3–49–1; Bright, 12–4–20–2.

Second Innings

G. Boycott, c Marsh, b Bright	29
J. M. Brearley, lbw, b Lillee	13
D. I. Gower, c Border, b Bright	23
G. A. Gooch, b Bright	21
M. W. Gatting, b Bright	39
P. Willey, b Bright	5
I. T. Botham, c Marsh, b Lillee	3
C. M. Old, c Marsh, b Alderman	23
J. E. Emburey, not out	37
R. W. Taylor, lbw, b Alderman	8
R. G. D. Willis, c Marsh, b Alderman	2
Extras (lb 6, w 1, nb 9)	16
TOTAL	**219**

Fall of Wickets: 1–18, 2–52, 3–89, 4–98, 5–110, 6–116, 7–154, 8–167, 9–217, 10–219.

Bowling: Lillee, 26–9–51–2; Alderman, 22–5–65–3; Hogg, 10–3–19–0; Bright, 34–17–68–5.

AUSTRALIA First Innings

G. M. Wood, run out	38
J. Dyson, b Old	1
A. R. Border, c Taylor, b Old	2
R. J. Bright, lbw, b Botham	27
K. J. Hughes, lbw, b Old	47
G. N. Yallop, b Emburey	30
M. F. Kent, c Willis, b Emburey	46
R. W. Marsh, b Emburey	2
D. K. Lillee, b Emburey	18
R. M. Hogg, run out	0
T. M. Alderman, not out	3
Extras (b 4, lb 19, nb 21)	44
TOTAL	258

Fall of Wickets: 1–5, 2–14, 3–62, 4–115, 5–166, 6–203, 7–220, 8–253, 9–253, 10–258.

Bowling: Willis, 19–3–63–0; Old, 21–8–44–3; Emburey, 26.5–12–43–4; Botham, 20–1–64–1.

Second Innings

J. Dyson, lbw, b Willis	13
G. M. Wood, lbw, b Old	2
A. R. Border, c Gatting, b Emburey	40
K. J. Hughes, c Emburey, b Willis	5
G. N. Yallop, c Botham, b Emburey	30
M. F. Kent, b Botham	10
R. W. Marsh, b Botham	4
R. J. Bright, lbw, b Botham	0
D. K. Lillee, c Taylor, b Botham	3
R. M. Hogg, not out	0
T. M. Alderman, b Botham	0
Extras (b 1, lb 2, nb 11)	14
TOTAL	121

Fall of Wickets: 1–2, 2–19, 3–29, 4–87, 5–105, 6–114, 7–114, 8–120, 9–121, 10–121.

Bowling: Willis, 20–6–37–2; Old, 11–4–19–1; Emburey, 22–10–40–2; Botham, 14–9–11–5.

England won by 29 runs.

Umpires: H. D. Bird and D. O. Oslear.

time. For sustained fascination, Test cricket is hard to beat; and this game was, in my experience, the equal of any in which I have played.

Our selection was relatively straightforward. We expected a better pitch at Edgbaston, and Willis confirmed during the week that it was likely to be flat and dry. Pitches rarely break up there: we have known the ball to turn, but never quickly. In the Test against India in 1979 Phil Edmonds made several balls spin sharply on the Saturday evening, but on Monday the ball went straight on. Bernard Flack's pitches rarely have much bounce for the quick bowlers either, though cloud cover may allow swing and seam movement. Old took 7–54 in the match against Pakistan in 1978.

We decided to leave Dilley out, despite his batting and his general ability. I was to tell him that the selectors had every confidence in him, and we hoped he would be back during the summer. We included him in the twelve, partly to keep together the side that had come back with such spirit at Leeds, partly to have him bowl in the nets at us and see if, together, we could help him back to his earlier accuracy. As it happened, however, he threw his shoulder out at Derby on the Monday, so we called Hendrick up to join the squad. We should have liked to play two spinners; Underwood was again discussed, but we could not imagine either going in with only two seamers or leaving out a batsman and having Emburey at No. 7. Our only other change was in the batting order. We decided to give Gooch some breathing-space away from the new ball. Gower was in good form and regularly bats at No. 3, so our early order would read: Boycott, Brearley, Gower, Gooch. The danger that Boycott and I might both get stuck and score too slowly seemed a less damaging prospect than losing a potential destroyer of the bowling to the new ball.

The weather on Wednesday was perfect for the royal wedding. I listened to the later part of it on my way up the motorway, and heard Milligan describing the occasion.

Perhaps having his ticket would have meant having his duties, too! As soon as I arrived, I looked at the pitch with Willis and Boycott: it was dry. Boycott's eagle eye noticed the matt of fine grass, and he suggested that I ask the groundsman to take more off. Captains can, I suppose, try to cajole a groundsman into changing his final preparations; and, knowing full well that the last cut has been carried out, I have sometimes as a joke asked when he intends to mow the pitch. But no self-respecting groundsman would be open to influence, and attempts to do so are extremely rare. Certainly Flack's pitch looked good to me, and I was not inclined to make any suggestions. Batsmen are notorious for having green-tinted glasses (or contact lenses). There were also fine cracks in the pitch, and one could move the earth between the cracks with one's hand: this suggested both uneven bounce and the chance of turn later. However, I thought it would be a good pitch for batting. This time there was no need for debate about who should be left out (Hendrick) or what to do if we won the toss (bat, in the knowledge that there would be some movement on the first morning).

Middlesex had again had an unhelpful gap in first-class fixtures; we had had only two one-day matches since the last Test. No wonder Test batsmen and spinners lose form during an English summer! I was therefore keen to have a long net against some fast bowling. Willis recommended the artificial pitch, and I had an excellent half hour with him and Chris Lethbridge, a bowler on the Warwickshire staff. These pitches enable one to play shortly after rain and to bat with confidence against quick bowling. The rarity of reliable practice pitches is a scandal in top-class cricket in England and elsewhere.

Back at the hotel, we gathered at the usual time for our pre-Test dinner. We started the team talk with a long conversation about our relationship with the media. Before Headingley Willis had told me that in his opinion the press were more hostile than when I had last played, and immediately after it had publicly slated the press for their 'smallminded quotes from players under pressure'. I too had at that time started my press conference with a blast against them for the way they had dealt with the question of Lillee's shirt-changing.

Before I had left Headingley, Peter Smith, the *Daily Mail* correspondent, had asked to talk to me on behalf of the cricket writers. He pointed out that they could do nothing about headlines, which came under sub-editors' jurisdiction. With regard to Willis's argument, Smith reminded me that there was nothing new in this procedure. For years, many papers had carried a 'stringer', a second writer whose job was to seek quotes and secondary stories from a big sporting occasion. Requests for interviews were always channelled via captain or manager, and were made only to players who had had a good day. Moreover, many cricketers used newspapers, writing articles or giving exclusive interviews for money. While stressing that some players felt that they had been unfairly and unkindly treated over the past months, I could acknowledge the force of Smith's arguments. And when I arrived at Edgbaston they were reinforced from another direction when Peter Lush, the publicity officer for the TCCB, sought my support in persuading the players to co-operate with the press in the interests of the general coverage of cricket.

At the team dinner I expressed my view that our vehement articulation of some part of our feelings had done no harm. The media should realise that players can be hurt by their reports. I too would prefer it if sports writers trusted their eye and judgment to describe the contest as they saw it; but the popular papers had for years lived off quotes and chit-chat, and occasionally we could help them to write the truth. Moreover, we were, as Smith had said, prepared to make use of the press when it suited us. I did not think that we should refuse to play the game altogether. I guaranteed that I would never try to force anyone to talk, nor would

I ask them to do so except when they personally had done well.

Boycott reckoned that the TCCB had us in a dilemma; they wanted us to talk yet if we put a foot out of line we were up before the Disciplinary Committee. Look at Willis, he said: fined £25 for commenting on local radio before the Lord's Test that the captaincy was affecting Botham's form. (Incidentally, a sympathetic supporter sent Bob the money to cover the fine!)

Botham himself was still simmering over the injustices he felt he had suffered while captain. He was also piqued by a report about the party he had held at his home on the Saturday evening of the Leeds Test. The story suggested that the England players had given up, and portrayed Botham dancing with Willis – a symbol, perhaps, of imperial decadence. More generally, Ian, who is a direct man, could not understand how someone could smile to his face, write vitriol, and expect to be welcomed back for more. He had been outraged, for example, when one reporter had asked Liam, then aged three, what Daddy ate at home. He now reacted to all this by refusing to talk to the press during the Edgbaston match.

When I went round the table, however, everyone else was prepared to co-operate, provided the requests were not too frequent. And three days later Ian had a talk with Smith, after which he too agreed to go along with these little interviews.

There will, of course, always be tension between performers and critics. Things tend to look easy from a distance, and criticism can readily become withering, professionally if not personally. One particular comment during the Headingley Test sticks in my mind. When Dyson – top scorer for Australia in both innings – was out in the second innings, Tony Francis on ITV news described his shot (to my mind a perfectly respectable one, similar to that which had produced four runs the over before) as 'this pathetic offering'. But it is equally characteristic of the potential explosiveness of relationships between performers and critics that this is the phrase that I remember rather than more reasonable and generous descriptions.

Cricket was also on our agenda at the meeting. We stressed, mainly, the need to start this match with the same aggression as we finished the previous one. We vowed that we would take the field expecting to bowl the opposition out in three or four hours. We would forget later fatigue; if by chance they survived our onslaught we'd find the resources to keep going. We encouraged Willis, Old and Botham to run in with all the fire they could muster; I wanted the same motivation and involvement from the fielders, however long we were out there.

I reiterated my views about no-balls, and pedantically reminded everyone that, with no rest day and with hot weather forecast, sleep and rest were essential. We talked much less about the Australians individually. We knew little of Martin Kent, who was expected to take Chappell's place, except that he was a flowing off-side player. Botham thought he was vulnerable to the short-pitched ball (but he tends to think this of any opponent).

Perhaps the team talk helped to maintain our recently-achieved high level of out-cricket. We said nothing about our batting; and this was what let us down at Birmingham.

As Hughes and I walked out to toss in the bright sunshine, there was already an eager air of anticipation around the ground. Union Jack flags and T-shirts, bought for the wedding, were much in evidence. Kim said, 'It's nice for the country to have something to celebrate.' As I won the toss, and said we would bat, I hoped we would give the country more to celebrate by the evening.

Lillee's first over was uneventful, except that a couple of balls kept so low outside the off-stump that they failed to carry to Marsh. After six balls, Lillee kicked the ball back down the pitch in disgust. Certainly there was no bounce to speak of. However, Alderman in particular bowled beautifully for an hour and forty minutes. He would smile, distractingly, as he reached the crease, a grimace of hunger rather than a gesture of affection. His line and length that morning were unwavering, and he achieved just enough movement, either way, to make life awkward. Lillee was less accurate. Early on he strayed to leg; as often happens, the ball would not swing for him when he set it off towards the leg-stump, though occasionally it curved sharply away outside off. We had scored 29 without too much anxiety when Boycott followed a good delivery from Alderman to give Marsh a comfortable catch. He was thinking of running it past gully.

We had a difficult time of it until lunch. Boycott, Gower and Gooch must all have been very close to LBW; and I played and missed several times outside off-stump. The jinx on the No. 3 position continued. At the meeting the night before Gower had asked, in a rather prickly tone, what the batting order would be. I had not appreciated that he would be unhappy about his move from No. 4 to No. 3; I ought to have explained the reasons for the change to him privately and listened to what he had to say. Now Alderman bowled one of his rare bouncers, just outside off stump. Gower went for the pull, mistimed it, and gave an easy catch to Hogg, playing in place of the injured Lawson, at mid-on. We were 29–2, and another No. 3 was out for nought; the series of No. 3s had now scored 88 runs in their last seventeen innings. Next match, we would ask the scorecard printer to enumerate the position between 2 and 4 '2a'!

Gooch looked confident, and drove Hogg – who replaced Lillee – for two fine fours. In between, Hogg bowled some fast and devastating balls, but had some trouble with his run-up. I had been stuck on 13 for over an hour, but got away at last. Ten minutes before lunch Gooch stepped back to force Bright on the off-side. The ball kept low, and he tried to check his shot. Bright appeared to hear nothing, and nor did I; but the close fielders appealed with unanimous conviction, and umpire Bird gave him out, caught behind.

Gooch's dismissal may have been related to an episode that took place a few minutes before involving Wood and me. I had edged Alderman to first slip. Wood claimed the catch, but I stood my ground. The fielders appealed and Hughes came up from slip to announce that Wood had caught it. Eyeball to eyeball, I said, 'I'm sorry, I thought I saw it bounce.' Bird consulted with Don Oslear, who had no hesitation in giving me not out. At the end of the over, Marsh muttered something about their fellows not claiming a catch when the ball had bounced, unlike us in 1978–9, which I took to be a reference to a catch Taylor claimed in a Test at Sydney. I am sure Taylor believed he caught it fairly, but a puff of dust showed, on the television, that he had been wrong. Watching the action replay of my incident, I cannot be sure whether the ball bounced or not; if I had to guess, I would say that it did. I do know from just one or two experiences in almost twenty years of cricket that one can be falsely convinced that one has made a clean catch. I was not implicitly accusing Wood of cheating by awaiting a decision.

The score at lunch was 68–3. Afterwards, batting was much easier. Alderman lacked his earlier nip and tended to over-pitch. Hogg was less quick. Lillee began to vary his pace to try to make something happen. Briefly I enjoyed myself; but after we had added another 33 I tried to drive a wide half volley from Lillee and edged it to second slip. It was a bad shot, though Lillee deserves some of the credit for a slower ball, bowled with an off-break action.

Half an hour later Gatting went in similar fashion, slicing a wide ball that was nearly a half volley hard in a direction that is usually vacant between slips and gulley. On this occasion, however, Lillee had Alderman, the third of his slips, wide, where he pulled off a brilliant catch diving to his right: 126–5.

Willey, now joined by Botham, had mixed watchful

defence with some solid blows, including a fine shot off the back foot through extra-cover. Lillee, ever resource-ful, tempted him to try this again. The ball bounced more and came in from the off; Willey lofted it slowly back down the pitch. Lillee, following through away from the pitch, turned back and just failed to hold the low chance. Though he did not bowl at his best, Dennis continually made the batsmen think. At the other end Bright had returned for a second spell, again bowling over the wicket. When the score was 145 he bowled a ball of a fullish length to Willey, pitching several inches outside the leg-stump. The batsman went for the sweep, the ball landed in the rough, turned and hit leg-stump: 145–6.

We needed Emburey to stay with Botham, and were aided by a dropped catch at slip by Wood. Botham, meanwhile, played some splendid strokes, including an uncharacteristically delicate little sweep off Bright. His dismissal was also uncharacteristic. He seemed to change his mind against Alderman, decided to play defensively and was bowled through the 'gate' for 26. If my lip-reading is correct, Alderman, asked by Lillee what happened, said, 'He just missed it.'

The tail folded without much resistance, though Willis played two of his unique sliced, inside-out drives over the off-side. The innings closed with a marvellous catch by Marsh, springing to his right like a big cat.

We had batted badly, especially after lunch. All the main batsmen had played themselves in then got them-selves out. Oddly, Botham, seventh to go, was the first man to be out from a defensive stroke – to which his comment was, 'I should have belted it!' We were very disappointed to have scored only 189.

Alderman was again the best bowler with the remark-able figures of 5–43 from 23.1 overs. He now had 25 victims in just 3½ Tests, a fantastic record. Before lunch he took 2–9 in eleven overs. His grouping in that first spell was remarkable, virtually every ball, as was shown by the small red marks on the brownish pitch, landing in a narrow strip about nine inches wide and three feet long on a perfect length around off-stump. Hogg, commenting on this after close of play, said, 'So that's where you're supposed to land them, is it?' Hogg had reacted to his no-balls in the opposite way to Willis, cutting down his speed of run-up and ending up bowling neither fast nor accurately.

Another reason for the low score may have been our sense of relief at playing on a flat pitch. Half-consciously, we may have wanted to produce carnival cricket to match the flag-waving post-nuptial atmosphere of the day. We threw away wickets gratuitously. Sir Leonard Hutton's suggestion, that batsmen play less well these days because they are worried about losing the £1,400 fee for the next Test, seems less likely. Money is the last thing one thinks about at the crease. Besides, bad thinking and bad shots have always been part of the Test scene.

However, the day was not yet over. In eleven overs we had Australia pinned down at 19–2, of which ten were extras, Old taking both wickets in five overs for only 1 run. He is a similar bowler to Alderman, without having quite his height or bounce. On the day's performance there was little to choose between them. The ball that bowled Dyson snaked back sharply to hit middle and leg-stumps, while Border, in trouble against Old, edged him faintly to Taylor. Exposing Border so early in the innings is the price Australia had to pay for having Kent replace Chappell.

In only 80 overs, twelve wickets had fallen for 208 runs on a good pitch. The weather was perfect for batting.

Friday morning was cloudier, a change that we welcomed. The ball, however, seemed to swing less than on the previous day. Wood, the remaining opener, had been joined by Bright. I decided to open with Old (from the City End, with the wind blowing from mid-on) and Emburey. I fancied the off-spinner's chances against Wood, and, wanting Old to have the first use of the more helpful end for seamers, I had to keep Willis back.

Old bowled superbly again, but this time without luck. Emburey was a little loose to Bright, straying down the leg-side. He was conscious of not having had match practice recently, and stiffened up between spells. I brought Botham on for Emburey and Willis for Old, Bright having steered two fours between slips and gully. At 62, Botham dismissed Bright for 27 with a ball dug in very short that failed to bounce. Bright had played a typically useful knock.

Botham, forever the optimist, tested Hughes and Wood with a bouncer apiece: both went for fours. I brought Emburey back at the Pavilion End. Hughes had the better of this contest until the off-spinner deceived him with a perfect floater which he tried to sweep but missed. He must have been perilously close to LBW.

At lunch Australia were 111–3. Both batsmen were well set, getting their noses right over the ball. The next session was full of excitement and incident. We were always on the alert for run-outs when Wood was batting. Indeed, he had got off the mark the night before with a single to Gower so short that Dyson would probably have been out had Gower's return hit the stumps. Now he hesitated for a fraction of a second before setting off for a short single to Old at mid-off. Old was quick to the ball, and threw down the stumps. Umpire Oslear, in exactly the right position, gave Wood out. I confess that at the time I thought Wood was in; but the action replay showed that the umpire had made a brilliant decision.

Now Yallop came in. We placed a very attacking field – silly point, two short-legs, three slips and a gully. Yallop looked amazingly jittery, so much so that Hughes turned down long singles to protect him from Willis, a ploy that should, I thought, have embarrassed any top-class batsman. Willis was charging in, as at Headingley, and the crowd roared him on. He bowled several no-balls (he was responsible for 28 altogether in his 19 overs): and now Hughes and Bird added to the strange tension that suddenly gripped the game. Hughes started by mouthing words (to whom, I don't know), letting two short-pitched balls hit him and swishing air-shots after others had gone by. Finally, having edged Willis just past second slip for four, he clapped ironically against his bat as he ran down the pitch. Dickie Bird also got excited and flapped off to square-leg to seek moral support from Oslear – for, presumably, a warning to Willis. The support was lacking, and the lonely Bird, shoulders hunched like a barn owl's, trudged slowly back to his post.

It was all somewhat mystifying. Willis certainly put tremendous effort into this spell, and could easily have hauled us back into a position of parity. But the batsmen survived and the next dismissal required another courageous decision by Oslear. Old was now bowling at the Pavilion End. Hughes pushed forward to him, bat hidden completely behind his front pad. The ball moved in from the off, and hit him near his left ankle. It would, I think, have hit the stumps. The question was, had Hughes played a shot at it? If not, the fact that the ball probably struck him outside the line of the stumps would not of itself preclude an LBW decision. Many umpires would have opted for the less controversial decision, giving the batsman the benefit of any doubt, and concluding that Hughes had, however tenuously, tried to play the ball. Oslear, rightly in my view, reckoned that he had not.

Old had one ball left of his over, which would also be Kent's first ball in Test cricket. Between us, Old and I made a mistake that cost us dear. We decided that there had not been enough bounce to justify having a short square-leg with the old ball: better, we agreed, to stop him squirting a single out on the leg-side. The very first ball Kent, nervously forward, played off bat and pad in a gentle lob to where Gatting should have been.

His off-the-mark shot was equally fortuitous. He tried to pull a Botham bouncer, and like Gower hit the ball high on the bat. Unlike Gower, Kent luckily scraped it past mid-on for 2. From then on, however, he played excellently, probably the best innings of the whole match. He drove the seamers handsomely through extra-cover, while against Emburey he made room to hit off either foot on the off-side. And he had plenty of time for his strokes.

His nerves – if that is the explanation – showed themselves in his running and calling (or rather, not calling). First with Yallop and later with Marsh, he managed to choreograph stops, starts and reversals which almost resulted in a pair of run-outs, each by about five yards. On the second occasion, Kent was halfway down the pitch when Gower lobbed the ball towards Botham, by now close to the bowler's stumps; however, Kent was lucky enough to be hit by the ball, and escaped.

Yallop's eventful innings ended with the score at 203 when he was yorked by Emburey; it was the first time John had ever taken his wicket. Emburey also first pinned Marsh down, then, soon after tea, bowled him as he tried to cut a straight ball. 220–7.

Willis was now bowling again, and Lillee's arrival sparked off more shenanigans. Lillee once again started to make room to cut Willis, but looked uncomfortable whenever the ball was bowled short outside leg-stump. There was some sort of collision between batsman and bowler as Lillee completed a single, followed in the next over by an outrageous no-ball by Willis. Umpire Bird looked anxious; had words with Lillee; hunched his shoulders.

Willis had already told me that he finds it hard to bowl at Dennis; he could not put his finger on exactly why. He thought it went back to 1974–5 in Australia, when he himself was batting and Lillee let go a ball that sizzled past his head as he lunged forward. Greg Chappell had then come up and implored Bob not to keep playing forward: they were helmetless days. Perhaps Bob knows that Lillee is a good enough batsman to warrant bouncers, but fears in his heart that he himself is not good enough to avoid Lillee's!

Meanwhile Kent, with his inward, controlled look and the bearing and beard of a Florentine prelate, was calmly going about his job. At 253, we had a stroke of luck. Emburey, who had been aiming more and more towards leg-stump, to avoid Kent's strength, veered wider than he intended, and Kent picked the ball up cleanly, clipping it hard towards deep square-leg, only to see Willis make a fine running catch.

Lillee was now charged up, as a result of his confrontations with Willis. In the same over, he pushed forward to Emburey; the ball turned and lobbed off his pad to Gatting at short-leg. Gooch, eager at silly mid-off, cried, 'Catch it,' but no one appealed. Lillee took exception to Gooch's exclamation, and then to Taylor's intervention. He struck the next ball firmly to me at wide mid-on, called Hogg for a single to try to keep the bowling, and Hogg was run out without facing a ball. Five minutes later, Lillee tried to hoik Emburey out of the ground and was bowled.

Australia were all out for 258, a lead of 69. Our bowling and fielding, which had been full of aggression, much of it well-directed, had put us back into the game. But we still had a crucial hour before the close.

In the dressing-room I spoke sharply to players who were chattering about the excitements of the previous hour. I needed to unwind from the concerns of fielding and reorientate myself towards batting. Boycott and I needed our precious five minutes of peace.

Back in the middle, neither Alderman nor Lillee swung the ball at all. It was Alderman's turn to drift towards the leg-side. Lillee's adrenalin was clearly flowing, probably an aid to him rather than us. He bowled quicker than in the first innings. In his third over, he bowled me an attempted bouncer which cut back and kept insidiously low. I was plumb LBW. Lillee raced up and vaulted the stumps.

Gower played some flowing strokes to reach his 2,000th run in Test cricket. Shortly before the close the day's play had a final twist of tension when the Australians thought they had him caught behind off Hogg. Wood made his feelings succinctly known from near the stumps, and Hughes asked the umpire why he hadn't given Gower out. (To which the only answer could be that he wasn't sure Gower had hit it.)

We ended the day at 49–1, just 20 runs behind. Runs had come more freely than on Thursday, 288 being scored off 88 overs. Still, it was surprising that ten wickets had fallen.

Kent and Marsh came into our dressing-room. Marsh asked me, sympathetically, 'You didn't expect yours to bounce, did you?' I asked if he had thought his would turn. 'I don't know what I was thinking,' he said.

The game was fascinatingly poised; but of course I was disappointed to be packing my bat away with three days still to go. In the morning I gave everyone a break from fielding practice, hoping that we would not be fielding that day. We did our usual exercises with Thomas on the far side of the ground. For the second time, Boycott arrived just after we started, to warm applause from the enthusiastic crowd and extravagant salaams from the rest of us. Afterwards I took the opportunity of having a look at Taylor in the nets. Talking to him the previous day I had realised that he was having a bad run with the bat and lacked confidence. He was particularly disappointed at having missed a perfectly straight ball in the first innings. I noticed that his first movement, against quick bowlers, had been slightly back towards square-leg, which made him late getting into line. Ironically, it was not until a week later that, while watching videos of the third and fourth Tests, I discovered that I too had fallen into this disastrous habit. Physician, heal thyself. At least I was able to offer Bob some remedial treatment, throwing a few balls to him from halfway down the net.

Back in the dressing-room we talked about the day ahead. Boycott said, 'We win or lose the match today. If we bat all day, we'll be able to set them a decent total.'

Hughes started with Bright bowling at the Pavilion End, into the breeze, and Lillee at the far end. After a few balls I found the intense glare irritating, and spent most of the morning watching on the television screen inside the dressing-room. We signed sheets of autographs, I remember, and chatted desultorily, but mostly, we watched on the screen the tense struggle taking place through the window.

Bright and Lillee bowled superbly. After Gower's problems at Lord's it was a good move by Hughes to open with Bright. Besides, if he could close up one end the seamers could be kept fresh by taking turns downwind. The move worked better than they could have imagined. First Gower was well caught off pad and bat by Border. Then Bright tied down both Boycott and Gooch to such an extent that in two hours he bowled sixteen overs for only 13 runs. He achieved his successes during this match, as in others during the series, mainly by bowling over the wicket and aiming at leg-stump. I could not agree with the 'traditionalists' who talked as if Bright ought to be a doddle to play from over the wicket. He drifts the ball in, and bowls from close to the stumps, so LBWs are by no means ruled out. He was accurate, giving the batsmen very little wide of the off-stump. When he pitched outside the leg-stump, aiming for the rough, which is usually evident by the second innings of a Test, the only stroke was the sweep. But except for a genius like Knott it is hard to be sure that one can keep the ball on the ground and cut out the risk of it bobbing up off the glove. Intikhab, Benaud and Gifford have all proved difficult to play when using this method. In 1977 Underwood made an important contribution to winning the Manchester Test by going over the wicket in the second innings. I have long thought it should be tried more often.

There was much criticism, especially of Boycott, for our defensive approach on Saturday. The *Sunday Express* headline read 'Disgrace! Boycott to blame.' Perhaps

Gooch should have played differently; if it had been a county match he would certainly have tried to hit Bright over the top. Had he done so at a crucial stage of the Test, and been caught off a mis-hit, the same critics would have blamed him for being irresponsible. My view is that it wasn't the defensiveness that was to blame; rather, we lost wickets unnecessarily after lunch. Instead of being, say, 130–3, we were 115–6 by mid-afternoon. No one blamed Randall for being too defensive when he scored 150 in ten hours at Sydney, or Boycott at Nottingham in 1977 when he took three hours to score his first 20, but went on to make an invaluable century. And later in this Test Border, the best of the Australian batsmen, scored 13 in 2½ hours, and played pretty well.

Certainly the belief that sport should be constantly exciting is a misconception, for which the media must take some blame. The tense cricket at Edgbaston was greeted by jeers from some of the same mouths that had an hour or two before so enthusiastically acclaimed Boycott and the rest of us.

Boycott's end came when Bright turned one sharply from about off-stump to take the outside edge. Not long after, Gooch tried to on-drive a quicker one and was yorked. We were now 98–4. The procession continued when Willey played exactly the shot that the bowler wanted him to play – an on-drive to a ball pitching in the rough just outside leg-stump. He was bowled by Bright for the second time in the match. Finally, Botham got himself out at the other end, wafting at a wide ball from Lillee. As he put it, 'My boots were filled with concrete.' At 115–6, we were a mere 47 runs ahead.

After lunch I had gone upstairs to have my ankle strapped by Thomas, a precaution we had been taking since the previous Saturday when I had turned it over while jogging on Hampstead Heath. For a change, I watched the cricket from that level. The glare is less trying when one looks down on the field; but the erosion of our middle order depressed me. When Willey was out

I ran downstairs to tell Old to put his pads on; perhaps he would be able to knock Bright off his length.

Gatting had been playing resolutely, apart from an attempted sweep that went via bat and pad, almost within Kent's reach at slip. When Old attacked Gatting too became more positive.

In 27 minutes the game was temporarily transformed. Old went down the pitch to Bright and hit him over extra-cover for four. When he bowled wide of the off-stump Old dragged him to long-on; then hit an even wider ball just in front of square-leg for another boundary. Sensibly, with the field well back, Old nudged the ball behind square and the batsmen ran two. Gatting took most of Lillee meanwhile, and the pair added 39 before Old, facing his first ball from Alderman, who had replaced the spinner, played across the line, and edged low to Marsh. Bright returned, probably to Emburey's pleasure; but Gatting became the third – of his eleven victims thus far in the series – to be bowled behind his legs while sweeping: 167–8.

So our brief revival had faded. We were still only 99 runs ahead, and the game looked ripe for Australia's plucking. Emburey knew, of course, that he had licence to play strokes, with only Taylor and Willis to accompany him. During the tea interval we agreed that his best chance lay in attacking Bright. When play restarted I stayed in the dressing-room, not wishing to show my face to outsiders. We again watched the game on TV.

Boycott started to talk to Botham about the lift to Doncaster he was hoping for after the game. Botham asked if he was happy being driven at 150 mph. Boycott, laughing, made some comment about 'his amiable gorilla', but pronounced the middle word 'ay-my-able'. Gower said, 'Ay-what? Do you mean "amiable"?' Boycott took the correction in good spirits, saying, 'I'm no cleric. I'm just your batsman-fielder.'

This exchange lightened our mood, and for the next few minutes Boycott amused us with tales of Brian Close.

He started with the stories, no doubt apocryphal, of Close's notorious driving habits; how on narrow winding lanes he manages to steer with the *Sporting Life* in one hand and a cheese sandwich in the other; and how on motorways he is alleged to take but a rare glance at the path ahead. No workman, sipping an honest mug of tea in a hole in the road, can be safe when Close is at the wheel! We got Geoffrey talking about Close's captaincy. He said it was a common thing for batsmen who had played a stupid shot to leave the field by another gate and dodge round behind the pavilion to escape the captain's wrath. In one match at Swansea Yorkshire had a dreadful session on the field, missing about eight catches, of which Close's share was three. In the dressing-room Close was going on about the fielding, and asked Boycott what he'd been doing when he missed his chance in the outfield. Apparently Geoff muttered to the effect that the captain should take a look at his own fielding; whereupon Close was alleged to have hung Boycott from a hook. 'I shut my eyes,' he said, 'and waited for the end.'

Emburey and Taylor, meanwhile, were delaying our end. Emburey swept Bright twice, then, with his curious short, stiff-armed swing, hit him handsomely back over his head. In five years, Emburey has turned himself into an extremely useful batsman. He is a shrewd cricketer, described on his début by Michael Carey, who was then writing for the *Observer*, as an embureyonic (*sic*) Titmus; and, like his predecessor, he makes use of every ounce of his ability. Taylor joined in with a nice off-drive off Lillee. When Bright went round the wicket for a few balls Emburey danced down the pitch inside the line and drove wide of long-off. They were not separated for an hour after tea; then Alderman, with the second new ball, took the last two wickets quickly, Willis again being magnificently caught by Marsh. The ninth wicket pair had amassed our only 50-partnership of the match, enabling us to reach a total of 219.

Australia's bowlers, Lillee and Bright in particular, had

performed excellently, and were well supported in the field. Marsh was impeccable throughout the match. Not only did he take seven good catches, but also dealt admirably with the awkward bounce and turn from outside leg-stump during Bright's 46 overs.

Their batsmen's nerves, on the other hand, were clearly jangling as they tried to survive that unpleasant forty minutes before close of play, and Wood lost his last contest with the umpires in this match when Old swung one in to have him LBW in much the same way that he had been out at Leeds. Border and Dyson hung on grimly, Willis extracting amazing lift from the dead pitch to take Dyson's gloves twice – but each time the ball went just out of Gatting's reach.

After nine overs, the close of play score was 9–1. In six hours 179 runs had been scored and ten wickets had fallen. I had had virtually nothing to do, but felt drained. After we changed, there was as usual a crowd outside the dressing-rooms waiting for autographs. I always like to be comfortable when I sign, preferably seated in a deckchair in the evening sunshine with the autograph hunters in an orderly queue. This was out of the question in the narrow thoroughfare at Edgbaston, so I sat on a plank of wood on the floor. People were encouraging; many of them fully expected us to win next day. I was more doubtful; lightning doesn't, does it, strike twice? 'To lose one parent, Mr Worthing, may be regarded as a misfortune; to lose both looks like carelessness.'

I put in an appearance at the Cornhill drinks session after signing. Cornhill came in on a five-year agreement as sponsors of English Test cricket when the Packer threat emerged in 1977. It has been a mutually beneficial arrangement. One aspect of the deal was that players would be prepared to do their bit at the receptions after close of play. Personally, I found them a chore. However nice many of those present may be, the players tend to huddle together defensively, and one rarely has a good conversation. Besides, half the people present would

Willis was unlucky in the first innings at Headingley.
Hughes's reactions were pretty quick in self-preservation.
He made 89.

A moment of realisation and delight. It *wasn't* a no-ball.
Willis bowls Bright to win the Headingley Test.

Boycott hugs his 'amiable gorilla'. Botham was named man of the match at Edgbaston after his final spell of 5 wickets for 1 run.

A typical Lillee appeal. Boycott is the batsman. Lillee enjoyed his usual controversial exchanges with the umpires.

Botham crashes a ball through mid-off for four during his great second innings century at Old Trafford.

Botham bowling at the Oval. Despite injury he got through 89 overs and took ten wickets in the match.

The perfect fast bowler's action. Lillee is the finest bowler I have played against. In the final Oval Test he had his best Test performance (7 for 89) and took eleven wickets in the match.

Marsh is well placed but Gooch is yorked by Bright in the Fourth Test.

Marsh appeals against Boycott. Bright got one to turn sharply.

Marsh batting at the Oval. Knott sent champagne to Marsh at Headingley when the latter passed his world record for Test victims.

Alderman listens to Lillee's advice. They finished with a combined total of 81 wickets in the six Tests. Alderman was the most successful of all bowlers in the series.

Bright has given me too much room for Hughes's comfort at silly-point.

Walking off at the Oval after my last Test innings.

have been drinking steadily since lunchtime. There would be a sprinkling of ex-players, some of whom we suspected of thinking that the quality of play had declined dramatically since their day; and there would also be pressmen hanging around for snippets. I would prefer to sign autographs!

The rest of the evening I spent with my sister and her children, and arrived back at the hotel to find Botham talking Gatting into going out to pick up some take-away Chinese food. We could lie in next morning, as play on a Sunday would not start until 12.00.

The morning was again sunny and warm. Another large crowd included many stripped to the waist. (That is, down to the waist, a necessary clarification, as at least one man I know responded at a medical to the instruction to strip to his waist by taking off his trousers and pants. We had no streakers at the Tests this year.) My plan was to give Bob a burst from the City End, and start with Old at the other end. I wanted Chris to have a chance with the new ball, but suspected that he would not find much help on this brown, fourth-day pitch. I expected Emburey to be our trump-card, bowling into the same rough that Bright had exploited, and only wished we had Underwood as well. For the quicker bowlers we planned to keep a third man at all times, to stop thick edges from racing for four. On such a slow pitch edges were not likely to carry to third or fourth slip.

Willis was magnificent. Of course the main difference between the two sides became, as the series went on, Botham's revival as the best all-rounder in the world; but almost equally vital in our success was Willis, who was the only bowler at Leeds, Birmingham and Manchester to attack with true pace. Now, on the deadest of pitches, he bowled like a man inspired. First he dismissed Dyson, whom he forced on to the back foot, with a ball that kept low. For Hughes we put two men back on the boundary for the hook, keeping Gatting at short square-leg. The presence of the close fielder makes some batsmen re-

luctant to eschew the hook shot, for fear of lobbing the
ball up off splice or gloves while playing defensively. For
once the ploy worked nicely, Hughes timing his hook
perfectly so that it carried all the way to Emburey fielding
a few yards in from the edge just behind square. There
was no one I could have preferred to see waiting for such
a catch, and Emburey caught it nonchalantly. This wicket
meant that Australia were 29–3, with Willis still fresh.
Yallop was very lucky to survive against him. The first
ball he received shaved his off-stump; a little later a ball of
similar length lifted to take the shoulder of Yallop's bat
and soar over the slips for four. Border had meanwhile
been struggling gamely, Willis forcing him back; now
Bob drew him forward, he edged the attempted drive,
and it flew low straight to me. I thought it would not
carry, but it did, and crept through my hands.

That seemed disastrous at the time, with Australia on
39, although both batsmen continued to be in difficulties
against Willis and Emburey. One ball from the latter
bounced and turned, but we had no gully to take what
would have been a dolly catch. Yallop chipped another
ball off the leading edge over mid-on. A catch off pad and
bat seemed a constant possibility. I kept Willis going for
twelve consecutive overs. Perhaps this was too many but
Headingley was fresh in our minds, and he still seemed
capable of a wicket. At last I took him off. I switched
Botham, who had bowled a few mean overs in place of
Emburey, to the other end.

Gradually, Border and Yallop became freer. The score
at lunch was only 62–3; we had kept them to 53 runs off
30 overs. Border was 13, after 2½ hours at the crease.
After lunch, however, there was the one brief patch in
which batsmen were in the ascendant. Old looked steady
but nothing more. Willis at last looked ordinary, and
Yallop took two consecutive boundaries off him down to
long leg. I gave him only three more overs in this spell.
Emburey was our main hope, and he bowled beautifully.

At last, the ball bounced right for us. Yallop tried to

ENGLAND v AUSTRALIA 1981   4TH TEST

4TH DAY	BOWLERS				BATSMEN					AUSTRALIA 2ND INNINGS					
	Umpires: BIRD PAVILION END		OS LEAR CITY END		SCOREBOARD LEFT			SCOREBOARD RIGHT		NOTES	END-OF-OVER TOTALS					
TIME	BOWLER	O.	BOWLER	O.	SCORING	BALLS	6s/4s	SCORING	BALLS	6s/4s		O.	RUNS	W.	L BAT	R BAT	EXTRAS
					KENT	23	1	MARSH	5	1	M24 NB 13	58	114	5	6	4	14
3:50			BOTHAM	10				... W	8	1		58	114	6	6	4	14
51								BRIGHT							0	
53		.		10				W	1	-		58	114	7	6	0	14
54								LILLEE							0	
55		.		10				. .	2		M25 4HR→	59					
56	EMBUREY	19			2 . . 1	27		. .	4		† stumping appeal	60	118		9	1	
4.00		.		11	. . . . !	32		.	5		† excellent stop (Gower)	61	119			2	
04	.	20						. . . .	11		M26	62					
07		.	″	12	. . . .	38					M27	63			.		
11	.	21						 1	17			64	120			3	
13		.		13	)			. W	19	-		64	120	8	9	3	14
14								HOGG							0	
16		.		13	)			. . . .	4		M28	65					
19	.	22			. . ! †	42		. .	6		† run refused	66	121		10		
23		.		14	1 . W	45	1				† run refused	66	121	9	10	0	14
24					ALDERMAN										0	
25		.		14	. . W	3	.		6	-	M29 NB/13	67	121	10	0	0	14
4.27	ENGLAND WON BY 29 RUNS										415 balls		ALL		OUT	

© BILL FRINDALL 1981

BOTHAM'S MATCH-WINNING SPELL
- 5 WICKETS FOR 1 RUN IN 28 BALLS

play his favourite on-drive against Emburey, edged the ball against his pad, and it bounced gently up to Botham at silly mid-off: 87–4, and a wicket had fallen on the number that is unlucky in Australian eyes, 13 runs short of 100.

Kent looked fairly comfortable, but Emburey now gave him nothing outside the off-stump. Border had not been well that morning. In fact, Hughes had made an unusual request before play; he came to our dressing-room to tell me that Border's stomach was queasy. 'If he's taken short while batting, would you be willing to wait for Border to come back?' My response was that this was an unreasonable request; if a batsman is forced to leave the field he has to retire 'hurt' or 'ill', and cannot come back until the fall of a wicket. Boycott and Botham shared my view.

I added that I wasn't even sure whether the umpires would countenance an unscheduled hold-up even if we agreed. Kim accepted this amicably. Border was un-shaven and grim – but neither feature called for a medical explanation. It was certainly a vast relief for us when he was out, caught off a freakish ball that bounced steeply to hit his glove.

At that point, the score was 105–5. I had been uncertain who to bowl at the other end from Emburey. Botham was strangely diffident. He felt that others should bowl before him; the ball was not swinging or bouncing – he wondered how he would get anyone out on this pitch. At his suggestion, I had just signalled to Willey, down at deep square-leg for Emburey, to loosen up. 'Anything's worth a try now,' Botham said. 'At least it's turning.' Two balls later Border went, and now I was confident that Botham should bowl. 'Keep it tight for Embers,' I told him.

Botham followed part of my instruction. In 28 balls he was hit for only 1 run. In this 40 minutes he also took the last five wickets. There was no trace of the Sidestep Queen now. To Marsh he started round the wicket, as indeed he had done earlier to Yallop and Border. This approach is not so valuable when the ball is swinging, as the chance of LBWs is virtually ruled out, but when it is not he often bowls faster, as he has to follow through straight in order to avoid running on the pitch. His first ball to Marsh, which was almost a yorker, nearly got through as the batsman played towards mid-wicket. Next ball was faster; Marsh again drove across the line, missed and was bowled middle-stump.

Bright came in with the score 114–6. Botham, charging in, surprised him with sheer speed. He was plumb LBW, first ball: 114–7. Lillee almost edged the hat-trick ball. He stayed for a few overs, but managed only three singles before Botham had him caught, at the second attempt, by Taylor, a replica of Botham's own dismissal 24 hours before. The score was, amazingly, 120–8; now we could offer Kent singles until the end of the over, and attack Hogg. For the first time I felt confident that we would win. Kent tried to drive Botham to leg, aiming I suspect for a 2 between the deep mid-on and deep mid-wicket. He missed, the ball brushed his pad and hit the off-stump.

This last day was played throughout at high tension. The crowd of 10,000 who, unlike the last day's crowd at Headingley, had paid the full admission charge, alternated between hushed silence and great roars of encouragement and approval. In this last dramatic act, they bayed Botham on. With the flair that makes him a great cricketer, he sensed his chance and grabbed it. Each time he took a wicket, his arms reached up, his chest filled, waist drawn in: a picture of exuberant triumph. It took him only three balls – all of which beat Alderman – to finish Australia off. This time he raced down the pitch, grabbed a stump, and holding it high sprinted from the arena.

Five wickets had fallen for only 7 runs! We had won by 29 runs.

'Keep it tight for Emburey,' I'd told him. I could never be quite sure that Ian Botham would do what I said!

7

Interlude

The experiment in Sunday play in Tests in 1981 was inconclusive, largely because in two of the three trials the matches did not last beyond the Sunday afternoon. Neither team had spent long enough in the field to be in need of a rest day, which would, as it turned out, have disturbed the continuity and unity of the match. Another advantage, from a personal point of view, was the opportunity the early finish offered for a few days' holiday in Wales. The weather continued to be idyllic, at least until Thursday morning, when storms flooded much of England and Wales. In the meantime I was able to sunbathe idly in a remote cottage garden, my eyes rising from the tunnel of laurel through the hazy heat and up to the rim of the mountain. I even took a languid scythe to the thistles and nettles that pass for lawn. In the evenings there were the stone walls and the lingering smell of wood-ash; and calls from my neighbour Ivor, a shepherd, who talked of the need for work to bring out a man's inventiveness.

Selfishly, I was not sorry that I need not race down motorways for a game of cricket on the Wednesday. There is, as Ivor says, more to life than play.

Wales offered, apart from its intrinsic delights, a sanctuary from telephone and mail. In the brief eight weeks from 7 July to 1 September in which I was again England's captain my mail was substantial; I should think I received at least fifty letters a week over this period.

Many referred to the enormous pleasure people had derived from the matches. There were occasional hints of an awareness that the dramatic and precarious successes by the national team had some intangible effect on national morale. Unemployment was, after all, approaching three million; and urban riots reached a frightening level in the summer of 1981. Shortly before the Headingley Test I was a guest at Westminster School's Foundation Dinner, where a fellow guest, Enoch Powell, and I found ourselves at cross purposes in a conversation on the subject of psychodrama. I thought he was talking about the media when his actual subject was *The Medea*. Not far away real life violence was being enacted from which we would, I think, have drawn different conclusions: it was that night that Brixton was sealed off by the police. Masters in evening dress had phone calls from anxious wives warning them about their journeys home. The anachronism of the occasion, in which guests are welcomed in Latin and Greek epigrams (translations provided) became pointed as reports came in of the scale of riots just two miles away. Were the inner cities to be torn apart? What medium of reconciliation had the Government or the country to offer? I was reminded of the day when the first big IRA bomb went off in Whitehall, and of the passage in *The 900 Days* in which Harrison Salisbury describes how in 1941 the inhabitants of Leningrad going about their innocent Sunday morning activities – setting out for an athletics meeting, going to visit a sick child, playing toy soldiers (White Russians against Red) – had their world shattered by the discovery that their country was at war.

Fortunately, these comparisons were largely of my own making. Perhaps it is also fantastical to surmise that so trivial a thing as cricket could have any impact on the explosive antagonisms within society. And yet the riots did subside. Possibly the royal wedding gave some sense of identity and romance to alienated sections of the community. And this fairytale event was flanked by two miraculous national successes, the third and fourth Tests. It is not fanciful, certainly, to claim that these wins gave a lift, however fortuitous and irrelevant, to the lives of millions.

My letters mostly expressed the personal aspect of this uplift. But one card read, simply, 'A wonderful tonic for England in these hard times.' 'People keep writing us off,' went another. 'But they need not, while cricket continues.' There was virtually no explicit reference to the riots, though one correspondent from Edge Hill in Liverpool speculated that the cause of the non-delivery of an earlier letter of his to me may have been the destruction of a riot-area postbox. Another exhorted Boycott to 'take his riot-guard off his arm as he only has *one* ball to hit!'

The cricket helped people in difficult personal predicaments. A girl of seventeen who had been unable to find a job after leaving college wrote, 'The cricket has kept my spirits up and stopped me getting bored. I don't know what I shall do when it's over.' A lady who needed something to help heal the hurt after the shock of her sister's death started watching cricket at this time, and thanked us for the pleasure the team gave her during the summer. A woman in Suffolk who had spent all summer in bed following a nervous breakdown found that it was the cricket, which she loves, that really helped her get better. And a widow who lives alone was 'just praying she would not have to go into hospital for her operation before the last Test'. An author put off serious chemotherapy treatment until after the series was over. The treatment worked well, too, when it happened!

A lady of 78 wrote, 'Hasn't it all been wonderful? I've watched every ball.' And a man thought that Leeds and Birmingham represented a hundred years of Test cricket at its best: 'The England XI represents every player in the country, and we are thrilled to bits to be represented by such a team.' These matches had caused work to be 'all but abandoned' in one office in Stenhousemuir, and a colleague who would 'normally only manage "good afternoon" rushed in shouting at me that there were eight wickets down!' A girl from Alderly Edge said, 'It always amazes me, at Test matches, how members of the crowd become so friendly with each other despite the different backgrounds and cultures.' One ten year old was won over to cricket: 'I have wrote also to Robin Jackman I said in the letter I don't like cricket much I love it now.' The age-range is wide. An 'anonymous London nonagenarian' congratulated and thanked us for having kept the Ashes. He remembered K. S. Ranjitsinhji 'with his billowing silk shirt sleeves', C. B. Fry, G. L. Jessop: 'I think it was Jessop who at Old Trafford once refused to bat against a namesake of yours whom he accused of bowling at his head . . . All of which reminds me as a schoolboy staying in the north with a friend one summer day, and upon entering Old Trafford the crowd, who evidently thought he fancied himself, were chanting as he came in:

> Do you mean to tell me you don't know me really,
> For I am the famous Walter Brearley.'

On the other hand, I also received a letter, fired by patriotic zeal, of which the following is part: (it was written on the first day of the fifth Test) 'Mr Brearley, at the time of writing, England are 175–9. Mr Brearley I am asking you, pull this team of yours round – You see, none of you care, do you? You don't care, none of you . . . Haven't your team got any pride in England . . . If you can't beat this Australian team, Mr Brearley, you can't beat anybody. They are a parks pitch team.'

Many letters were more personal. Already in June one writer exhorted me to 'march breast forward into the next England selection committee meeting and announce your availability. This is no time for faint hearts. Grasp the nettle in both hands, look Bedser in the eye and say "I'm your man." The whole nation will rejoice.' Not quite. Ian Todd in the *Sun* wrote that making me captain and No. 3 was not only a selectorial disaster, it was nothing less than an insult to Ian Botham. And one of my correspondents quoted the 'admirable' Italian proverb: 'If you want to know a fish is bad look at its head.'

Many of the letters were touching: a woman, plucking up the courage to send in her first radio play, told me that she would not have taken up writing if it had not been for me. I do not know how I had been instrumental in changing this stranger's life, but I was. This reminded me of another occasion on which I unwittingly exerted a distant but significant influence: a university lecturer, whom I had never met, faced by a difficult and sub-versive group in a faculty meeting of which she was chairman, heard my voice instruct her, clearly and aptly, to 'ignore the buggers'. From that moment her career has never looked back.

A former friend of Wilfred Rhodes and a 'fanatical follower of Test cricket since 1921' wanted to enlist as a patient of mine, although his purpose in doing so was perhaps betrayed by his going on to say, 'I could bore you with data such as Maurice Leyland's 133 in the Roses match of 1924.' A Surrey supporter, less bravely, sug-gested I put Graham Roope on my couch once I was fully qualified: 'I cry when he comes back to the Oval pavilion after fretting and strutting for a mere 14 or 42.' (Roope, when I told him this, was not so keen!) In the last of these letters about psychology, a correspondent referred to a cricket match played at the Maudsley hospital in the 1940s – Freudians v Jungians; 'this was won, alas, by the Freudians, owing no doubt to our missing some subtle sexual implications of their strategy, and ponderings over the symbolism of the red ball slowing down our reaction time.'

My mail was a constant seesaw of compliment and complaint. In case I should believe that I was a 'wizard, John Merlin Brearley, responsible for the transformation of the team', I should read the following curt letter written after Edgbaston: 'Dear Brearley, why not do England, Middlesex and yourself a favour – opt for non-playing captain?' This sentiment, which reminds me of the backhanded compliment on a large poster in Australia, which read 'Brearley for Governor-General', overlooks, I think, the physical closeness of a captain to his players, essential in the field for fully understanding the players' states of mind and keeping them on their toes.

One of the wittier – and friendlier – letters came from a 'drunken sick bed' in Cardiff, warning me that its owner was 'taking legal advice over my sufferings occasioned by your captaincy. First, as a result of Headingley and Edgbaston, I have had two heart attacks. Second, I had only just sobered up after Leeds, and here I am back on the bottle again.'

The same correspondent who quoted the Italian proverb went on to describe it as a master-move to bring back Knott (for the fifth Test) to keep wicket to Underwood, and then drop Underwood. He ended 'Yours speechlessly'. I also enjoyed a letter to the *Guardian* which might have ended 'Yours ambiguously': 'On Friday I watched J. M. Brearley directing his fieldsmen very carefully. He then looked up at the sun and made a gesture which suggested that it should move a little squarer. Who is this man?'

People wrote to me also about the other players, and there was no shortage of evaluation and advice. Gooch was 'a great lump of nothing', and Tavaré either the hero or the villain of the Old Trafford Test. Knott's physical jerks seemed to evoke surprisingly strong feelings of antipathy or affection, while Dilley's gestures to the crowd called forth one request that he should make the 'ultimate sacrifice' and resign forthwith from Test cricket (and that I should congratulate him on his withdrawal with 'a few suitable classical words'). Not even Botham escaped censure. One man enquired from Broadstairs after Ian had finished off the Edgbaston Test, 'Why is it that he is always put on to bowl at the tail-enders? And why is it when an opposition batsman is caught or bowled Botham always runs up before you (the captain) to congratulate the player involved, surely your prerogative?' (The answer, I suppose, is that he runs faster than me).

And one observer asked, 'Must Botham, a most refreshing cricketer' – the understatement of the year? – 'spit every minute of the game? The slips must be knee-deep in expectoration.' I was bidden not to pick my nose in public. Finally, Boycott and Gower called forth this poem after Edgbaston:

> Boycott and Gower in the pavilion sit,
> Instead of cricket learning to knit.
> On a batting wicket balls they cannot hit.
> Surely on this form they ought to quit
> Instead of chewing gum a baby's tit
> And to a jumble sale give their cricket kit.

Much kinder was the 'Old Timer' who wished me the best of luck back as England captain. He had some excellent tips, too; 'Keep the players happy,' he wrote, 'and get them confident. Get their brains working with good team work, but keep happy and contented. Have faith in yourself and the players that they can do it.'

There was no shortage of tactical advice. We should for example reverse the batting order. A more sensible suggestion was that our batting order should be flexible. When Gooch and Boycott opened I was told, 'You should go No. 3 if the score is more than 50 when the first wicket falls. If more than 50, but less than 100, you bat if Boycott is out, Gower bats if Gooch is out.' There was more along similar lines, and it makes excellent sense except for the fact that players prefer to know when they will bat, partly for superstitious reasons and partly because it is easier to relax when one is not next in. Occasionally I do adopt this writer's ideas, but rarely.

One man, perhaps living in the past, urged me to get to know which of the Aussies didn't like googlies; others wished that I could stop the fielders hugging and kissing.

I have had huffy letters from colonels in Surrey about this 'palaver'. 'Dear Brearley, must we have all this hugging? Is not taking wickets and holding catches what you chaps are paid for? The captain's hand on the shoulder and a quiet "well-caught" should suffice. Yours etc . . .' Behaviour that seems outlandish to such writers feels quite natural to us. Cricketers in the 80s are less inhibited than their predecessors in the 50s. In 1977, during a stoppage for rain, we watched a film on television of Jim Laker's match at Old Trafford in 1956. After a few dismissals Derek Underwood, incredulous, said, 'But they don't seem to be pleased about taking wickets!' Their reactions looked, to our eyes, rather low-key. The bowler might allow himself a modest hitch of his trousers as he sauntered down to a group of fielders whose 'creams' were unlikely to be sullied by any mark of mud or grass. It was all in a day's work.

We are, on the whole, much fitter than Laker and his contemporaries. But not all of us live up to one writer's expectations, that we 'should be as physically fit as Larry Holmes, Geoff Capes or Superman and mentally alert as any Genius, Einstien (sic) etc.'

A Bedfordshire man wanted to help us to deal with balls passing the off-stump by recalling his uncle's method. This energetic relative 'had a bat specially made for him on which the curvature was the same on both sides. When he received a ball outside the off-stump he struck it with extreme velocity, reversing his swing, through or over the slips' heads either for four or more usually for six.' Perhaps this letter was meant for Willis, who could accommodate it within his present style with less modification than most.

I have changed my method of dealing with the flood of letters which can seem so engulfing. I always reply to requests for autographs that contain stamped addressed envelopes, but not always to others. I am now aware of my own need for time and space. The pile of mail from strangers – requests and offers, advice and enquiries,

letters of adulation and of hatred – is daunting. Sometimes the contents are bizarre, as in one begging letter
from Bangladesh whose writer thought it high time, as
'the British people are still celebrating the royal wedding
and England registered their historic victories over
Australia, to get from my friends as gifts seven girls,
three Christians, two Muslims and two Jews.' They are
also charming (like the requests for autographs to 'hang
next to my bedraggled scoresheet from Leeds, which got
chewed during the last day's play'. But I will end with
those from the oldest and youngest of my supporters.
The former read:

Dear Mr Mike,
I thought I must write and congratulate you on being
captain for our English Team once again. Good luck.
I prize the photo of yourself you sent me on my 94th
birthday and soon will be 95 not out. I always watch the
Tests and keep the score. So good luck to you all –
                                    Florence Rapley.

And

Dear Mr Brearley,
I would like to offer myself as your youngest mascot.
I feel I must have brought you luck as I was born on the
day you won your match by 18 runs, came home on
your last match (and watched the final over with
Mummy and Daddy) and am exercising my lungs over
this present Test.
    I was delivered by a cricket-mad Australian Doctor
who insists I look like a future women's cricket Captain
(I have big hands and long legs – a wicket keeper
perhaps). I am small enough to fit in your case if you
decide to tour this winter. Good luck.
                                    Miranda Carreras
                                    aged 3 weeks.

It is pleasing to get such messages. It is also pleasing to be cheered by the crowds, as at Birmingham when a section of the crowd behind me sang 'Michael, row the boat ashore' during the final scenes of that saga. The heterogeneity of the views reflect, though, my own feelings about myself. The outcome was indeed agreeable; it was pleasant to bask in the glory of those two remarkable wins. Yet we could so easily have been 2–1, even 3–0 down. Kim Hughes might have been the celebrating hero, leading a side that had already completed its task and won the Ashes. Instead he had to face the cruel assaults of a disillusioned press, and imagine the reception he would receive once he was back home.

I reflected on the fine way in which he and the rest of the Australian team had accepted defeat. He was quite straightforward, as usual, in the interviews after the match. He felt sorry for their bowlers, who twice had put them in a winning position only to be let down by their batsmen. He anticipated the criticisms there would be about his own dismissal when he hooked Willis down the throat of long leg. 'You have to play it as you see it,' he said. 'I'm a natural stroke player; that time it didn't come off.' I agreed with him, and admired his dignity; he looked shocked, almost desolate. Yet within a few hours he, together with Lillee, Dyson and several others from their party, turned up with brave faces at a dinner dance in aid of Bob Willis. They had agreed before the match to appear for Bob, thinking no doubt that as it was in the middle of the Test they could justifiably leave early. In fact, though robbed of their excuse, they were marvellous. Kim kept saying, 'I suppose me mum'll speak to me.' Pause. 'Reckon me dad will, too. And my wife.' Pause. 'But who else?' We had time to talk about the crowding of the calendar with Tests. He said that some of the Tests against India last season had felt less combative, less significant, than an inter-state match. Their players were jaded with constant Tests, double tours and one-day Internationals.

I enjoyed his company. I find it harder to be at ease with Dennis. He said to me, 'Come on, Mike, I'm only fierce *on* the field,' but I could only grin sheepishly. Both of them saw the party out, were lively and personable, pleasant to the people who wanted to say hello, or ask them for an autograph. I doubted if I could have enjoyed myself at such a function in Melbourne, had the roles been reversed.

Sometimes even the winners disappoint the public by appearing less ecstatic with joy than myth would have them be. I think there are two reasons for this: one is the sense of anti-climax – there can be nothing to match the exultation of the final moment in a close match just won; and the other is the awareness that for every winner there's a loser. That there, but for the grace of God, go we.

8

A Great Century

I drove home on the Thursday through torrential rain and floods in West London. The storms were country-wide. Though we did not know it until the day before the next Test, they had soaked the Old Trafford pitch. Our enquiries, made before the rain, led us to expect a pitch that could take spin. Its texture when dry is such that the follow-throughs, even if not the main part of the strip, can powder, offering some help to the versatile spinner.

For two Tests at least we had been wondering how we could fit Underwood in. It is almost unthinkable to go into a Test match in England with only two front-rank seam-bowlers, and the weather conditions alone can make a third essential if one is not to relinquish control. But to include a second spinner at the expense of a bats-man would mean an exposed tail with Emburey much too high at No. 7. England were to take this risk at Bombay later in 1981, and lose to India.

At Birmingham, Underwood's presence would have been invaluable; I was sure that the Australians, without the experience of either Greg or Ian Chappell, would not enjoy facing him. There was, I thought, only one way of getting Underwood into the twelve; and that was to pick Knott in place of Taylor. These ideas were forming in my mind while I was in Wales. I thought that I should find out more about the form of the two Kent players, and also of Chris Tavaré, so I phoned their captain, Asif Iqbal. He told me all three were playing well.

Underwood had by his standards been struggling for much of the previous fifteen months. He had last played for England in the Lord's Test in 1980, while in the middle

Fifth Test, Old Trafford, 13–17 August

ENGLAND First Innings

G. Boycott, c Marsh, b Alderman	10
G. A. Gooch, lbw, b Lillee	10
C. J. Tavaré, c Alderman, b Whitney	69
D. I. Gower, c Yallop, b Whitney	23
J. M. Brearley, lbw, b Alderman	2
M. W. Gatting, c Border, b Lillee	32
I. T. Botham, c Bright, b Lillee	0
A. P. E. Knott, c Border, b Alderman	13
J. E. Emburey, c Border, b Alderman	1
P. J. W. Allott, not out	52
R. G. D. Willis, c Hughes, b Lillee	11
Extras (lb 6, w 2)	8
TOTAL	231

Fall of Wickets: 1–19, 2–25, 3–57, 4–62, 5–109, 6–109, 7–131, 8–132, 9–175, 10–231.

Bowling: Lillee, 24.1–8–55–4; Alderman, 29–5–88–4; Whitney, 17–3–50–2; Bright, 16–6–30–0.

Second Innings

G. A. Gooch, b Alderman	5
G. Boycott, lbw, b Alderman	37
C. J. Tavaré, c Kent, b Alderman	78
D. I. Gower, c Bright, b Lillee	1
M. W. Gatting, lbw, b Alderman	11
J. M. Brearley, c Marsh, b Alderman	3
I. T. Botham, c Marsh, b Whitney	118
A. P. E. Knott, c Dyson, b Lillee	59
J. E. Emburey, c Kent, b Whitney	57
P. J. W. Allott, c Hughes, b Bright	14
R. G. D. Willis, not out	5
Extras (b 1, lb 12, nb 3)	16
TOTAL	404

Fall of Wickets: 1–7, 2–79, 3–80, 4–98, 5–104, 6–253, 7–282, 8–356, 9–396, 10–404.

Bowling: Lillee, 46–13–137–2; Alderman, 52–19–109–5; Whitney, 27–6–74–2; Bright, 26.4–11–68–1.

AUSTRALIA First Innings

G. M. Wood, lbw, b Allott		19
J. Dyson, c Botham, b Willis		0
K. J. Hughes, lbw, b Willis		4
G. N. Yallop, c Botham, b Emburey		0
M. F. Kent, c Knott, b Emburey		52
A. R. Border, c Gower, b Botham		11
R. W. Marsh, c Botham, b Willis		1
R. J. Bright, c Knott, b Botham		22
D. K. Lillee, c Gooch, b Botham		13
M. J. Whitney, b Allott		0
T. M. Alderman, not out		2
Extras (nb 6)		6
TOTAL		130

Fall of Wickets: 1–20, 2–24, 3–24, 4–24, 5–58, 6–59, 7–104, 8–125, 9–126, 10–130.

Bowling: Willis, 14–0–63–4; Allott, 6–1–17–2; Botham, 6.2–1–28–3; Emburey, 4–0–16–1.

Second Innings

G. M. Wood, c Knott, b Allott		6
J. Dyson, run out		5
K. J. Hughes, lbw, b Botham		43
G. N. Yallop, b Emburey		114
A. R. Border, not out		123
M. F. Kent, c Brearley, b Emburey		2
R. W. Marsh, c Knott, b Willis		47
R. J. Bright, c Knott, b Willis		5
D. K. Lillee, c Botham, b Allott		28
T. M. Alderman, lbw, b Botham		0
M. J. Whitney, c Gatting, b Willis		0
Extras (lb 9, w 2, nb 18)		29
TOTAL		402

Fall of Wickets: 1–7, 2–24, 3–119, 4–198, 5–206, 6–296, 7–322, 8–373, 9–378, 10–402.

Bowling: Willis, 30.5–2–96–3; Allott, 17–3–71–2; Botham, 36–16–86–2; Emburey, 49–9–107–2; Gatting, 3–1–13–0.

Umpires: D. J. Constant and K. E. Palmer.

England won by 103 runs.

of an unprecedented lean patch. And despite a good haul of wickets in August he had started 1981 without his usual accuracy. At his best, Derek's most unusual quality had been the speed at which he bowled – his stock ball being medium-slow, and his quicker ball surprisingly fast. Thus when he managed to make the ball turn even a little it would do so sharply. Batsmen have always found it hard to pick up Underwood's length and line early in flight: a feature he shares with other great spin-bowlers. Now Asif told me that he no longer bowled at quite his old speed, but that he had regained his accuracy and his confidence.

Both he and Knott had returned to form in the match against Middlesex at Maidstone, which started on 1 July. Alan had scored 100 runs in the low-scoring match, and played our strong seam attack with skill. And Asif said that he continued to 'keep superbly. Tavaré, too, Asif reckoned, would serve us well.

As England captain I took every opportunity to find out the opinions of those I respected about players who were in the running for a place. The information is usually disinterested: a captain's reluctance to lose a key player to the Test team is usually outweighed by his pleasure at seeing a colleague elevated. Players do sometimes over-rate their own team-mates, especially in Yorkshire where, however much they bicker among themselves, they keep a solid front of mutual esteem to outsiders. Criticism of Yorkshire is like criticism of one's own mother – permissible only to those born and bred there.

However, apart from Old and Boycott there were no Yorkshire players pressing for a place. The hard decisions concerned wicket-keeping. Bob Taylor had kept very well both at Lord's and Headingley, and though he had unaccountably dropped several balls at Birmingham he had not missed a chance. What is more, he had taken part in the 50 partnership with Emburey which had been as significant as any other episode in that match in our eventual win. It would be hard indeed to drop him. Nevertheless, I have always believed that if one can improve a side, however well it has done, one should. In my opinion, neither Knott nor Taylor is quite the 'keeper they both were in the 70s; but I have always felt that though it is Taylor whom one would choose as a model, Knott has in his unique way always been his equal as a 'keeper alone. 'Knotty' annoys the purists by taking the ball one-handed more often than Bob, and the public by the glimpses of obsessionality that he gives them with his exercises and rituals. But he believes as a matter of policy that it is often safer to take a low ball with just the one hand; and the fact is that he rarely drops it. As for the exercises – well, I would be happy for him to stand on his head between deliveries if he felt it helped. And what is publicly visible is only part of the story. Alan Knott has rules for diet (no cheese and meat at the same meal, for example); since hurting his neck in two car accidents a few years ago, he has had his driving seat specially remodelled to support him; and he is so chary about draughts that he would come away from a day's play in India wearing three sweaters, an anorak with its hood up, a scarf and dark glasses. Bob has never needed to go to such lengths. It is a mark, though, of the professionalism and superb skill of both these great players that they have so very rarely been unfit for a game.

For me, then, it is Knott's batting that tips the scales. Bowlers from Bangalore to Brisbane have been driven to distraction by his unorthodox brilliance. He has scored five Test centuries, and over a long career averages more than many specialist batsmen. If Underwood played, Knott would be vital; if not it would be comforting to know that a man of his mercurial ability would be batting at No. 8.

Our other bowlers – Willis, Old, Botham and Emburey – picked themselves. For his all-round performance in the fourth Test I would have made Emburey man of the match; but in the moment of triumph it must have been hard to go beyond Botham. For much of the match Old had been the pick of our seamers; his four victims were the top four in Australia's order. But what of the batsmen? It had been a difficult series for batsmen on both sides. There was a case for the omission of Boycott (not only for his slow scoring), of Gooch, who had looked uncertain against the moving ball, of Gatting, who had yet to make a big score at Test level, and of Willey, who like Gooch had performed with such courage against the pace of the West Indies. Even Gower had struggled, both against the quicker bowlers and against Bright. Yet was anyone else in the same class as most of these players?

Larkins had been the reserve opening batsman for the last match; and Tavaré had covered for Gower, Gooch or Gatting (if any of them had withdrawn, it was he who would have batted at No. 3). I was convinced that we needed a specialist No. 3, someone who relished the problems of that position. I think that it is in many ways the hardest place to bat. No. 3 misses the occasional loosener that comes the way of the opening batsman. By the time he bats, the bowlers have often discovered the right pace and length for the pitch. And ideally he has to be sufficiently versatile to cash in on a good start. England had lacked someone who filled this bill for many Tests. Tavaré himself had shaped competently there in two Tests against the West Indies but, like Woolmer, had been sacrificed on the altar of all-out attack against their fast bowling. He had, moreover, gradually improved in the last year. It was time to give him a chance. The question was, in place of whom? Reluctantly, we decided that Willey should go. Technically he was the most vulnerable of our batsmen and he had played two poor shots against Bright's spin to get out at Edgbaston. Yet he, like Taylor, would be very much missed. His Geordie wit and straightforwardness had picked up individuals and the team often over the previous two years. He was a professionals' professional.

So, at the end of a long meeting, we eventually opted

LURIE
THE TIMES

for three changes from the twelve picked for the previous Test: Knott for Taylor, Tavaré for Willey and Underwood for Dilley. I had the unpleasant task of phoning Bob and Peter to tell them the news. Bob has had enough disappointments over the years to take it graciously. Peter had already suspected the worst. During the dressing-room conversation while Taylor and Emburey batted at Birmingham, I had described how in 1976 after one Test I had heard that I had been left out for the second from the dressing-room attendant at Bath (falsely, as it turned out); and learned of my actual dropping a Test later over the radio. I thought this an unnecessarily unkind way of discovering bad news, so when I was captain I made sure that either Alec or I phoned the player concerned before the announcement of the side. Peter Willey, jokingly serious, had offered me his telephone number (as had Graham Gooch).

Before we split up, we tried to think of ways of helping our batsmen who had struggled so hard for runs. I asked John Edrich to talk to Gower about playing the spinner; John advocated more footwork, conning the bowler into changing his length, especially when there is rough outside the off-stump. We agreed to ask Underwood to bowl at Gower before the match. As for Boycott, Close in particular thought he should be more positive; I suggested that I should be the one to talk to him. Gatting we felt needed one breakthrough at top level: there was no particular advice we could give him – except to keep trying. Gooch had played better at Birmingham; he should be encouraged to play his natural game.

Somehow the *News of the World* found out the team changes and published them on the Sunday morning; what is more, they knew the exact voting (3–2) on the Knott/Taylor issue. The article went on to say that 'there's bound to be a wave of fury in the Midlands directed at Mike Brearley who, I understand, recommended the change.' This was ingenuous, since any wave of fury was possible only because of the publication of that very sentence. I phoned Bedser to complain about the leak; but we never discovered for certain its source.

We had another change forced on us as Chris Old broke down with an injured knee on Monday. The choice of replacement lay between Robin Jackman and Paul Allott. Those who had seen Jackman reckoned that his bowling lacked some of the life that he had shown the previous season and in the West Indies; so we picked the 24-year-old Lancastrian. Allott is tall (6ft 4ins), and strong. Clive Lloyd gave him long spells, and he had responded to this so well during the season that he had taken more wickets than anyone in the country except Richard Hadlee. Like Simon Hughes, he is a product of Durham University. The Australians too had to call up a seam-bowler, and at even shorter notice. Lawson was already out of the reckoning with his bad back, and at a late hour Hogg also withdrew. So they pulled in the 22-year-old left-armer mentioned to me by both Greg Chappell and Inverarity, Whitney. He had come to England to play in the Northern League. While he was there, Gloucestershire signed him on after Mike Procter's injury, and he was actually playing at Cheltenham against Hampshire when the emergency call came. I imagine that Graham Beard, the all-rounder in the Australian party, must have felt snubbed to be passed over in favour of a man who had played only six first-class games. No doubt either Thomson or Carl Rackemann, another Queenslander, would, if they had been fit, have been invited before Whitney. The fact that Beard came behind all of them suggests that his initial selection was a mistake. No touring team can afford to carry a player whom the tour selectors cannot trust to step into a Test in case of injury. They must have felt that Beard, who bowls at a gentle medium pace, would never be likely to be more than a stock bowler at Test level.

I first heard of Whitney's elevation at our team dinner on the evening before the match. (I had not been to the ground for practice, as I had a sore throat.) Gooch and

Gatting had both played against him, and they reported that he was quite 'slippery', but only slanted the ball across; they had not seen him swing it in. Before we sat down I told David Gower with a smile that he could go back to No. 4 now. I added that I had not realised that he felt so attached to that position. He said, 'But doesn't it make any difference that I was there first?' We had already announced that Gooch would be opening again now that Tavaré had come into the team. We needed to avoid having Boycott, Brearley and Tavaré together, a combination that could well clog up the innings. With Gower No. 4, Gatting No. 5, me No. 6 and Botham No. 7, there would, we hoped, be a happy combination of stroke-players and grafters.

I received various further pieces of intelligence about the pitch. Only then did I discover that it was not entirely dry, thanks to the previous week's rain. Moreover, the consensus was that it looked unevenly grassed. At one end there was, Botham added, a crack and a circle the size of a dinner plate which looked like the remnant of an old follow-through; both these factors might help the spinners.

We went through the Australian team man by man for the benefit of the newcomers, and repeated our exhortations to be aggressive with the ball; we should take the field expecting to have Australia out in, say, three hours. Willis remarked that he had often been spurred on by this sort of talk; what could we say that might give an equal boost to the batsmen, especially in the first innings? Boycott was curiously in need of reassurance: how much talk of changes in the batting had there been among the selectors? How did I expect him to play? I said that he must know better than anyone that each innings was a new start. Perhaps, I suggested, he should take the advice I had often heard him usefully give to others, to play positively whether in defence or attack. Hardly anyone, as he was aware, could be given total assurance about selection; all I could say was that it had not escaped the selectors' notice that conditions had rarely been good for batting so far.

After the meeting he and I stepped out into the forecourt of the eighteenth-century Mottram Hall Hotel and in the cool evening I tried to find out what was bothering him. I think that Geoffrey was, at last, very keen to tour India. He wanted to beat Sobers's record of runs scored in Tests – 8,032 – and to play in a series when he would be less of a target for 90-mile-an-hour missiles. And now, as the crucial time approached, there were voices in the press calling for his removal. What was more, he had been put on a United Nations Black List because of his South African connection. The suspicion must have crossed Boycott's mind that the selectors might ditch him so that they could go ahead with the tour without problems. I could merely tell him that I could not imagine the selectors doing any such thing; they most certainly were not gunning for him. I tried to encourage him towards a less anxious, less cautious frame of mind.

He put one record behind him early next morning; when he reached 7 he passed Cowdrey's aggregate of 7,624 runs in Test cricket, thus becoming England's highest Test scorer. The pitch had looked less scabrous after being cut and rolled an hour before the start. Chris Hawkins, the groundsman, reckoned that it would help the seam bowlers a little to begin with and the spinners at the end, but would not break up. The selectors toyed with the idea of leaving out a batsman, but we all returned to the notion that a draw would, after all, suit us better than Australia. It was the batting that needed to be bolstered, so Underwood was made twelfth man. Despite the overcast conditions I did not seriously consider fielding first; though Hawkins was probably right that the pitch would not crumble, there had to be some turn later.

Botham thought that Boycott had also been inhibited earlier in the series by being overconscious of the Cowdrey record; so we all hoped that passing it would

free him for a big innings. Not so. He edged Alderman on
to his thigh, whence the ball lobbed up for Marsh to dive
forward to take a fine, agile catch. Next over Gooch, who
had started confidently, was LBW to a ball from Lillee that
cut back off the pitch. We were 25–2. Tavaré at once
looked sound. He makes his intentions of coming forward whenever possible plain before the bowler lets the
ball go, his front foot creeping towards the bowler. But he
has time to duck the bouncer or play off the back foot.
Having the left hand behind the bat – a grip that does not
find favour in the coaching books – helps him to play high
in defence, a technique he, like Woolmer, learned from
Knott. Balls outside the off-stump he left strictly alone.
I used to think he was too static, almost mechanical, in his
play, which might make adjustments to the deviating ball
difficult. In these conditions, however, against some
more fine bowling by Alderman and Lillee, he looked
competent and solid. By mid-afternoon, Willis was saying of him, as he met yet another ball with the middle of a
defensive bat before setting off on his little walk-about
towards short leg, 'I *do* enjoy watching Tav bat.'
Similarly, front-row forwards, who like seam-bowlers
are the engine-room of the ship, appreciate safe, solid
kicks for touch from their backs rather than fancy play
which has them chasing back to their own corner flag!

Gower's genius tends, by contrast, to teeter on the
brink of the flamboyant, if not the fancy. Today he lived
dangerously, mishooking Alderman over Marsh's head
where Wood just got a hand to the ball as he ran back
from slip. Then, when the stocky Whitney with his Afro
haircut and belligerent air replaced Lillee, he flashed at
one outside the off-stump; the unfortunate Wood missed
the ball altogether with his hands but not his head, and
was for the second time on the tour taken to hospital for a
precautionary X-ray on his cheek. Twenty minutes later,
Gower helped rather than hit a similar ball from Whitney
to gully, where Yallop made no mistake.

With the score at 57–3, I went in ahead of Gatting,

hoping to steady the innings for a while, but lasted only a few minutes before being LBW to the first ball I faced from Alderman. Gatting, as often, looked solidly aggressive, a stand-in stuntman for Botham's Henry VII; but he failed to play the protagonist's part to the end. Having twice pulled Lillee for four he was unable to resist a high, loopy bouncer, finished the stroke too soon, and gloved the ball gently to slip. The stage was set for a royal performance as Botham made his entrance, loosening his shoulders with great circles of his heavy bat. This time he lasted only one ball; Bright, stationed fine and close in the gully for the off-side steer which Ian tends to play early in an innings, took a superb left-handed catch low to the ground. An excellent piece of bowling (by Lillee), captaincy and fielding.

We were 109–6, and pleased to have Knott coming in at this crisis to join his unflurried Kent colleague. Knott had been asking us if Bright swung the ball in from over the wicket – he can do; which makes his favourite sweep shot more risky. He was also anxious about not being able to leave the ball outside the off-stump. Batting at No. 6 – or lower – in county cricket, he had fallen increasingly into the habit of looking to score from anything wide.

He soon had the chance to sort out both preoccupations, with Bright bowling at one end and Alderman at the other. As he tried to do so, we noticed his mannerisms while batting with amusement: his face worked, his feet trod, and his bat was lifted awkwardly a little off the ground. Anyone who only saw Knott in crabbed defence would find it hard to believe that the impish genius on the attack was the same man. Now, however, he came down the wicket to pick the spinner up over mid-wicket, a shot that would be culpable in anyone but Knott. He failed to connect, but Marsh missed the stumping, one of his few errors in the series. Next over, Knott edged Alderman to second slip, where Border took the catch.

The light at this time was appalling, the scoreboard

lights beaming brightly from the other side of the ground. As Knott said later, 'I suppose if you don't play in gloom up here you'd never play at all.' And Old Trafford does have the best seeing conditions for batsmen of all the Test grounds, with its large sightscreens and the open sky beyond them.

When Emburey left twenty minutes later to a similar tame shot we were 137–8. In taking his third catch of the day, Border cracked a bone in his left hand. The Australians had had several casualties; apart from Wood and Border, Yallop had been off the field with a migraine, and Chappell later hurt a finger trying to catch Tavaré at third man. Tavaré had been the subject of ignorant barracking from some sections of the 18,000 crowd; now he improvised productively, stepping away from Alderman to hit him through the off-side. In an hour he and Allott added 38; with five minutes to go I was trying to catch Tavaré's attention to ask him to play quietly for the close when, forcing Whitney on the off-side, he edged him to Alderman who was now at first slip: 175–9. It had been an excellent innings, plucky and sensible. Whitney, too, would remember the day on which he played for Australia and took two for 31. No doubt he had at times found his task more gruelling in Sydney grade cricket.

Friday turned out to be one of the most extraordinary days in an extraordinary series. First, to the huge delight of a capacity crowd, England added 56 runs in only twelve overs for the last wicket, the local débutant almost doubling his previous best first-class score to end 52 not out. Hughes opened with Whitney rather than Alderman, a decision based, I imagine, on Whitney's extra speed. They may well have been forgiven for not knowing where Allott's strength lay, but it soon became clear that he liked the ball short of a length outside the off-stump. When Alderman came on, his first over with the new ball cost 16 runs, eight of them from a stroke known to me in my school days as the 'Chinese cut', an attempted forcing shot off the back foot on the off-side where the ball is edged past the stumps down to fine leg. Like most last-wicket partnerships, this one contained the usual mixture of the sublime and the ridiculous; to the Australians it must have seemed like further evidence of demonic bias, after the ill-luck of losing the previous two Tests.

Nevertheless, they would have settled, at the start, for bowling us out for 231, especially as the pitch was now dry and the sun was out. Willis beat Wood twice in his first four balls; the fifth was only just short, but Wood, already moving on to the front foot, swivelled and pulled high for four. The next one was intentionally short and faster; Wood hooked it for six. When Willis bowled again to him, we had an unconventional field of three slips, third man, gully and cover; wide mid-on, and two long-legs. Wood's approach, though I did not realise it then, was a pattern for what followed. He hook-pulled yet another four in Willis's second over.

As Willis began his third, Fred Trueman, broadcasting on Radio 3, was highly critical. He had Doug Insole, who well knew how rarely Trueman found cause to admire any English fast bowler since he himself retired, fuming in a London traffic jam. 'I should be ashamed to draw my pay if I bowled like this in a Test. The worst bowling with a new ball I have ever seen,' said Fred. In Bob's next six balls he took three wickets. First Dyson, who had been playing soberly enough, was out, like Hughes at Leeds; not quite over the lifting ball, he was caught low down at third slip. Hughes himself smashed his second ball, which was short, high over extra cover for four; but was at once trapped LBW well back on his stumps. And with his sixth ball, Willis found the edge of Yallop's bat and Botham caught his second catch – a marvellous, low, one-handed effort. When Allott, with the first ball of his next over, swung one in to Wood to have him LBW, the first four wickets had fallen in seven balls.

It was hardly surprising that a few seconds elapsed

before the next batsman, Border, emerged from the pavilion. The Australians must have been nonplussed. Such a collapse was almost incredible on so true a pitch.

The crazy pattern of the innings continued. Martin Kent in the midst of chaos played a gem of a knock, but even his strokes smacked of a desperate refusal to be shot down in a bunker. His 50 came from the remarkably low number of 42 deliveries. At one time we had three slips for him, and all other six fielders on the boundary. Botham, who was bowling, said to me: 'But I want to keep him attacking. If he does I'll get him out.' I replied, 'I reckon he'll still go for his shots with this field.' I was right; two balls later he was missed at third slip driving furiously at Botham. Before this, however, we had had another stroke of luck, though the catch that brought it was a brilliant reflex response. Just before lunch Border, who was in some pain, drove hard at a wide half-volley from Botham. It flew fast to fourth slip, where Gower, who was in close for the edge from a defensive shot, caught the ball above his head. The score at lunch was an improbable 58–5 from 11.4 overs.

Australia had clearly settled on a new aggressive batting policy for this Test, and it could so easily have succeeded. Instead many of their batsmen were out from their first error. Immediately after lunch this happened again; Willis bowled a good ball to Marsh, swinging away just outside his off-stump; the batsman withdrew his bat too late, and the ball ran off its face straight to Botham. At 59, Bright came in to play the longest knock of the innings. He helped Kent add 45 exhilarating runs, until in Emburey's first over Kent, who had already taken 6 runs from the over, tried to force a ball off the back foot and edged it to Knott: 104–7. Lillee stayed for 40 minutes, looking fairly safe, until Willis, whose fourteen overs had been interrupted only by lunch, was replaced by Botham. Ian's golden touch continued as Lillee immediately flicked a leg-stump half volley straight to Gooch behind square-leg. Allott at once fired in a leg-stump yorker to bowl Whitney, and Botham contributed a beauty to finish the innings off. 130 all out in 30.2 overs! Apparently it was the shortest innings by Australia in a Test since they were all out in 23 overs for 36 runs on a drying pitch in 1902.

Lillee and Alderman, who must at 12.30 have put on their nosebags eagerly, at 4 o'clock found themselves back in harness. I noticed in the first innings that Lillee had probed at Gooch's leg-stump, looking for one to swing and have him playing too square on the leg-side. Now Alderman succeeded with a straight ball that hit leg-stump as the batsman went too far over. Tea was taken with the score at 7–1.

On resumption, Boycott and Tavaré restored a sense of Test match normality. Geoff's effort to be more positive consisted mainly in pushing the ball into gaps and calling for quick singles, to which Tavaré responded sharply and well. Both played sensibly and the score was 70–1 at the close.

On Saturday morning, Botham and I went to the nets together. I said, 'You go in first, but you can't have half an hour.' He played a few speculative defensive shots, then some equally speculative attacking ones. He was out at least twice in a few minutes, and as usual the bowlers – Gooch and Emburey on this occasion – gloated. Whereupon he smote Emburey miles over the back of the stand. The ball must have landed among spectators – fortunately we heard no ambulance sirens.

Gooch said: 'Come on out, Wooden Top, that's enough of that.' As no one would bowl at him, Ian came out, disgruntled. Now he wanted to get his own back. Both is rarely keen to bowl in the nets, and when he does he often amuses himself with a succession of bouncers. This day was no exception. He bowled fast and well at me and then at Boycott. Having burned off some energy and regained face, he ambled off happily to the pavilion. His idea of batting practice before an important innings is simply to get his arms moving and feel the ball on the bat. He did the same on the Saturday morning at Birmingham, not being too particular about the quality of the bowling or of his strokes. When I jokily remonstrated with him, asking what good this practice was doing any-one, he responded by parodying his earlier play, his foot even further from the line of the ball.

The team were in good spirits that morning. 171 runs ahead, with only one wicket down, and the pitch looking good. True, the cloud-cover might give the bowlers a little assistance, but they had looked less lively the evening before. Yet just after lunch Australia had hit back with such effect that we had lost four wickets for only 34 runs in two hours twenty minutes' play. Tavaré was still there, but had managed only nine runs before lunch. It was desperately hard going. Alderman started the decline by producing a beauty to get rid of Boycott. Gower was unlucky, pulling a long-hop hard only to see Bright at square-leg hold on to it above his head, like a goalkeeper. Gatting, not learning from his first innings dismissal, was missed by Wood at slip, again hooking at a high Lillee bouncer; then, just on lunch, he was LBW half-forward to the persevering Alderman. Finally, I was well caught wide down the leg-side by Marsh. So we were 104–5, only 205 runs ahead, when Botham strode to the crease.

He played even better than at Headingley. Of course, the pitch was much easier, so there was no need for the heaves and slices that spiced that innings. At Old Trafford, Botham played an innings of classical power and splendour; of off-drives, hooks and cuts. He played soberly enough to start with, his first 30 balls producing just three singles. He began to open out against Bright, a cut for four being followed by a handsome lifted cover-drive for four. When he was 28, Australia took the new ball, and Botham murdered them. He hooked Lillee for three sixes in two overs. Two of these were extra-ordinary; both bouncers were exactly where Lillee in-tended, head-high and dead straight. Botham ducked his head at the last moment, went through with the stroke, and cleared the two long-legs by 30 yards. With two men back for the shot, were these hooks (like Hughes's at Birmingham) irresponsible? On the last tour of Australia many critics were saying that Ian should be told to control himself and play more responsibly. Would he have been foolhardy if he had marginally mistimed one of these hits and holed out on the boundary – a case of yet another English batsman falling for a simple Lillee ploy? Botham's genius enables him to get away with the foolhardy often enough for it hardly to be foolhardy at all.

Apart from the hooks, Botham drove Lillee back at about head-height so hard that the bowler was fortunate to be bending down in his follow-through. It reminded me of a day in 1963 when Wes Hall scored a hundred against Cambridge in 69 minutes, and Richard Hutton told me he wanted to follow-through backwards for safety's sake. 22 runs came off one over; at the other end, he pulled Alderman for a massive six over wide long-on; the ball was only slightly short.

Meanwhile Tavaré kept going with his vital innings, tortoise to Botham's hare – though he had to run like a hare in response to some of the latter's calls. 'I like batting with Tav,' Ian said afterwards. 'He seems to understand my calls even when I mean the opposite!' Later christened 'Rowdy' in India, because he talks so little, Tavaré is a good listener, and when he says no he means it.

Just before tea, when Alderman at last started to bowl at middle-and-leg to Botham rather than outside his off-stump, Ian played a couple of wild swings to leg. Boycott and Knott, who could tell the line of the ball from the television inside the dressing room, told me that they were too straight for the shots. I signalled to him to go easy; eight an over would suffice. As Knott said, the sky was the limit to what he could now score. It sometimes seemed rather to be his target.

Certainly Whitney must have felt that as he ran back from mid-off to catch a horrible, steepling skier off

IAN BOTHAM'S 118 AT OLD TRAFFORD

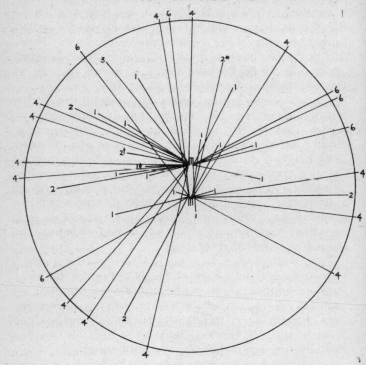

WARWICK ROAD END

STRETFORD END

Runs	Balls	Minutes	6ˢ	4ˢ
50	60	76	2	6
100	86	104	5	11
118	102	123	6	13

Bowler	Balls	Runs	6ˢ	4ˢ
ALDERMAN	17	24	1	3
BRIGHT	36	25	2	2
LILLEE	24	45	3	4
WHITNEY	25	24	-	4

BOTHAM'S SCORING SEQUENCE

000000110001000000000000000000
1104410410010100000042142*161642†
24041‡460020000406004300260000
10601400400 W.

N new ball taken at 3·37 pm (Botham 28 off 53 balls)
* dropped by WHITNEY at deep mid-off (off ALDERMAN)
† including one overthrow
‡ overthrow
W caught by MARSH off WHITNEY

© BILL FRINDALL 1981

Alderman's bowling when Botham was 32. And he gave another half-chance, to third man (no position is safe!), later on. Overall, though, his innings was a heady mixture of control, even culture, and massive power. He played himself in; then hit orthodox shots all round the wicket.

The party ended fifteen minutes after tea, when Botham, at 118, edged Whitney to Marsh. As the Australians clapped him out, their looks expressed a rare Antipodean awe at the prowess of an Englishman.

There was still time, though, for more champagne. Knott played a sparkling, scintillating innings of 56 not out, his 50 coming off fewer balls than Botham's. (When I mentioned this to Ian at close of play, and asked him why he'd hung around early on, he said 'See how long it takes him to reach a century, then.') We finished another extraordinary day at 345–7.

Sunday was a lovely day for cricket. My instructions were that we should try to bat at least until lunch. I remembered well India's coming within 8 runs of a target of 439 on a similar last innings pitch, at the Oval in 1979; Sunil Gavaskar scored a marvellous 221. I had been criticised there for not declaring earlier. Hughes had himself said that they had more chance chasing 500 than 150. From lunch on Sunday until the end of the match ten

Bill Frindall's run chart. Botham's innings contained a striking number of off-side fours. I can remember only one really edged – shot – registered on the chart as a four to the sight-screen at the Warwick Road end – when Botham, trying to force Whitney on the off-side, edged him just past the off-stump. Another striking feature is that Ian scored virtually no runs between the bowler and square-leg, the main exceptions being his amazing pull for six off Alderman and a straight six off Bright. A few more statistics for this innings. Botham went from 26 to 100 from 33 balls after Australia took the new ball. He went from 3 to 100 off a mere 56 balls. In the history of Anglo-Australian Tests no one has ever hit six sixes in an innings. It is hard to believe that any of us there will ever see a greater knock.

hours' play were possible, so even 500 runs would require a rate of only 50 an hour.

As it happened, Knott went early, caught by a brilliant one-handed dive by Dyson at third man as Alan played his favourite uppercut off Lillee. John Dyson had earned a voluble fan club at the Stretford End for his efforts on the boundary, culminating in this great catch. From 356–8 we did well to reach 400. Emburey played splendidly to reach his first half-century in Tests, while Allott again gave no-nonsense North country support. When we were all out just before lunch, Australia needed 506 to win.

To climb Everest you first have to get your expedition under way. Australia made their mountainous task more difficult by a wantonly poor start. However, if 100 is some sort of base camp, they reached it in the remarkably short time of eighteen overs, for the loss of two wickets. And with 40 minutes to go on a dazzlingly clear day, the summit was clearly visible and definitely within reach. The score was 210–3, and Graham Yallop looked utterly at home. By the close, however, Emburey had struck twice, and the target looked as distant as ever.

It was not entirely due to impeccable judgment that Wood had so far in the series run out only himself. Now Dyson, who was omitted from the team after this match, had the ladder pulled from under him as Wood sent him back too late. Gower was the fielder, assisted by Gatting who ran in from short square-leg to break the wicket; over the years he is only one of a number whom I have nagged into doing this automatically from the bat-pad position, as they can always get to the stumps sooner than the 'keeper, standing twenty yards or so back.

Wood followed soon after, attempting to hook an innocuous long-hop from Allott. He edged it to Knott, who took the low catch with two hands. At 24–2, Yallop joined Hughes. The left-hander had had a poor series so far, scoring 141 runs in nine innings. Another low score here would surely have meant the loss of his place for the

Oval, yet he went about the task with an assured confidence and a silky touch. More than most Test players, Yallop can range from the inept to the masterly. Often he looks ill at ease at the crease. As the bowler runs in he slides his back foot to and fro in a grandmotherly shuffle. If there is pace in the pitch, he is particularly vulnerable. But even then he rarely misses the chance of playing his pet shots, the cut and the straight drive, as well as fluent strokes off his legs. He is a top-class player of spin. On this occasion he must have decided that he would take on our quick bowlers, so whenever they dropped short he hooked or pulled. He was notably severe on Allott, punishing any deviation of length, and driving with a full flow of the bat.

Hughes, too, played well, though early on he was lucky with several forcing shots that only narrowly cleared the slips. At one point I put a man halfway to the boundary behind the fourth slip, but the ball kept going to either side. We may have had a large credit of runs in the bank, but I did not feel happy at the speed at which they were being used up. 100–2 off eighteen overs! This was a good scoring rate in a Sunday League match, let alone a Test.

At the drinks break in mid-afternoon it was announced over the public address system that I would captain England at the Oval. I had heard the news from Bedser earlier in the day, and was delighted to be able to finish the series. I knew that Ian still hoped to get the job back; covering up his ambition, he said as we poured down the glucose drinks, 'All names in the hat for captain in India by Friday, please.'

It was Botham who struck next; he caused Hughes to edge one just short of my right hand at slip, and then moved one the other way to have him LBW in much the same way that Gatting had been in our second innings. Each of them had now been LBW six times in five Tests. At about this time we had some light-hearted visitations from the crowd. A gorilla wanted to shake hands with

Botham, and two sinister-looking men in shirt-sleeves walked deliberately up to the stumps. We all watched in amazement as they quietly picked off the bails, turned, and walked back unhurriedly the way they came. 'We did it for a bet,' they said later. They were given bail.

Yallop and Border, unperturbed, went on without much trouble. Out of the blue, Yallop, on 89, edged Allott to Tavaré's right at first-slip where he just failed to hold the catch. Within a few minutes, Yallop hooked Botham for four to reach a fine century – off only 116 balls.

With 40 minutes left, and the score on 198, I tried Emburey for a second spell. His first ball was a low full-toss outside Yallop's leg-stump. The batsman missed the ball, it brushed his back foot and went on to the stumps. Emburey had now dismissed Yallop three times in four innings; this was the only time he had not earned his wicket.

The last period of play was crucial. We made a mistake that I was to repeat next day, of not having a short-leg for Border. He was understandably a little jumpy to the short-pitched ball, when one of our seamers got it exactly right, and two or three times in his long innings it hopped up off his glove to where short square-leg would have been. I realised too late, also, that Border does tend if anything to play just outside the ball, so he was more likely to give a chance on the leg-side than, say, to third slip. But there were many times over these last two days on which I needed an extra fielder or two; broken hand or not, Border hit the long hops hard on either side.

We had, however, learned one lesson at Birmingham: that Emburey should bowl at Kent's middle-and-leg. I felt we might catch him off pad and bat at silly mid-off if Emburey kept bowling the right line, and this happened a quarter of an hour before the close. I had taken over the silly mid-off position from Botham, who was increasingly finding that the constant crouching prevented him from getting the rest he needed for bowling. Marsh came in rather than Bright, and the two left-handers quietly played out time. Emburey's last spell of five overs brought him two wickets for six runs. The close of play score was 210–5.

Australia continued to fight hard throughout the last day. Marsh swung the bat in a variety of unconventional and more orthodox ways to score 47, and with Border took the score to 296 before Willis, bowling with the second new ball, had him caught behind. We had decided to try bowling a little wider of the off-stump to Marsh and were lucky that his first swish there took the edge. Invariably Willis seemed for some reason to find extra pace for Bright; soon he made one bounce to take the glove, and Knott took a good leg-side catch. It was now 322–7. Willis was tiring; while Bright brought out his best, against Lillee he again looked less dangerous. This time Lillee decided that the pitch was quiet enough to play him conventionally, getting behind the line and defending, rather than stepping back to the short ball and cutting. Border made our job harder by skilfully keeping the strike. I was always conscious of the clock, and the fact that the target was well under a run-a-minute; so after Lillee had played himself in I too was willing to play cat-and-mouse, giving Border long singles early in the over, and not over attacking Lillee.

Botham started to bowl the first two or three balls of an over to Border off a very short run. 'Bowl *properly*,' I told him. 'We've still got two slips. Let's try and get him out.' Ian muttered something about my not having to bowl 40 overs an innings; but his next ball was much faster. He would frequently ask me if I found it tiring, at my age, to stand at first slip. When at last he beat Border's outside edge, Knott and I could not remember the last time this had happened.

At last, Lillee became more adventurous, aiming to cut Allott. The ball flew wide of Botham at second slip, who flung himself up and to the right to bring off a wonderful two-handed catch. Five runs later, he charged in to have Alderman LBW. The courageous Border together with a determined Whitney kept us waiting for another hour before we finally knew that the Ashes were ours. During the tea interval the main scoreboard was evacuated following a bomb warning; when I sent Allott down to the boundary after tea, Boycott told him, 'I'll send your spectacles to your mum.' Emburey, who had earlier had Marsh dropped at deep square-leg by Gower, was un- lucky again when Border gave his only chance, which was missed by Knott. We had twenty-five minutes plus twenty overs to spare when Willis finally settled the series by having Whitney caught by Gatting at short leg. Border was 123 not out, and proved in this innings that he is one of the best players in the world. Australia had again fallen short of their target, but by contrast to the other two occasions how well they had batted. Only when Lillee was out could we be certain of not losing.

As in 1977, and again in 1978–9, we had won three Tests in a row against the old enemy. These three in 1981 more than compensated for the three lost in a row in 1979–80. From first to last, the matches had hung in the balance. They also, perhaps more than any set of matches in the history of Test cricket, depended on the prodigious achievements of one man.

9

Lillee's Last Laugh

The series that had risen from the ashes with its three blazing climaxes was now settled. The Ashes themselves were either retained (according to the official English view) or regained (as many Australians would insist), but on any reckoning secured by England. The sixth Test at the Oval proved, however, to be in no sense an anti-climax. In many ways it was more mature, less intense or hectic – less bizarre, even – than its predecessors, yet absorbingly interesting from beginning to end. It was fitting that Australia should end with the honours of the match, but pleasing for us to hold on for a draw.

There was much to play for. When Bedser asked me to captain the side for this last Test, he made it clear that a condition of my acceptance would be that I would not oppose an element of experiment in selection. He was keen that one or two of the batsmen who had been on the edge of the team all summer should have a chance now. At the selectors' meeting, we all agreed at once that Graham Gooch should be rested. In his case this was not a euphemism for being dropped into more or less a permanent oblivion; we knew that he would come back, but technically and psychologically he was not 'on song'. As a replacement, we considered Larkins, Parker and Geoff Cook.

Larkins and Cook, who open together for Northants, had become one of the most reliable pairs in the country. Cook was the steadier, and some felt the straighter batsman; but his career average of less than 30 counted against him. Larkins had played in five Tests, but never had a run of matches together, nor had he batted in his

Sixth Test, The Oval, 27 August–1 September

AUSTRALIA First Innings

G. M. Wood, c Brearley, b Botham		66
M. F. Kent, c Gatting, b Botham		54
K. J. Hughes, hit wicket, b Botham		31
G. N. Yallop, c Botham, b Willis		26
A. R. Border, not out		106
D. M. Wellham, b Willis		24
R. W. Marsh, c Botham, b Willis		12
R. J. Bright, c Brearley, b Botham		3
D. K. Lillee, b Willis		11
T. M. Alderman, b Botham		0
M. J. Whitney, b Botham		4
Extras (b 4, lb 6, w 1, nb 4)		15
TOTAL		352

Fall of Wickets: 1–120, 2–125, 3–169, 4–199, 5–260, 6–280, 7–303, 8–319, 9–320, 10–352.

Bowling: Willis, 31–6–91–4;
Hendrick, 31–8–63–0;
Botham, 47–13–125–6;
Emburey, 23–2–58–0.

Second Innings

G. M. Wood, c Knott, b Hendrick		21
M. F. Kent, c Brearley, b Botham		7
K. J. Hughes, lbw, b Hendrick		6
G. N. Yallop, b Hendrick		35
A. R. Border, c Tavaré, b Emburey		84
D. M. Wellham, lbw, b Botham		103
R. W. Marsh, c Gatting, b Botham		52
R. J. Bright, b Botham		11
D. K. Lillee, not out		8
M. J. Whitney, c Botham, b Hendrick		0
Extras (b 1, lb 8, w 1, nb 7)		17
TOTAL (9 wkts dec)		344

T. M. Alderman did not bat.

Fall of Wickets: 1–26, 2–36, 3–41, 4–104, 5–205, 6–291, 7–332, 8–343, 9–344.

Bowling: Willis, 10–0–41–0;
Botham, 42–9–128–4;
Hendrick, 29.2–6–82–4;
Emburey, 23–3–76–1.

ENGLAND First Innings

G. Boycott, c Yallop, b Lillee	137
W. Larkins, c Alderman, b Lillee	34
C. J. Tavaré, c Marsh, b Lillee	24
M. W. Gatting, b Lillee	53
J. M. Brearley, c Bright, b Alderman	0
P. W. G. Parker, c Kent, b Alderman	0
I. T. Botham, c Yallop, b Lillee	3
A. P. E. Knott, b Lillee	36
J. E. Emburey, lbw, b Lillee	0
R. G. D. Willis, b Alderman	3
M. Hendrick, not out	0
Extras (lb 9, w 3, nb 12)	24
TOTAL	314

Fall of Wickets: 1–61, 2–131, 3–246, 4–248, 5–248, 6–256, 7–293, 8–293, 9–302, 10–314.

Bowling: Lillee, 31.4–4–89–7; Alderman, 35–4–84–3; Whitney, 23–3–76–0; Bright, 21–6–41–0.

Second Innings

G. Boycott, lbw, b Lillee	0
W. Larkins, c Alderman, b Lillee	24
C. J. Tavaré, c Kent, b Whitney	8
M. W. Gatting, c Kent, b Lillee	56
P. W. G. Parker, c Kent, b Alderman	13
J. M. Brearley, c Marsh, b Lillee	51
I. T. Botham, lbw, b Alderman	16
A. P. E. Knott, not out	70
J. E. Emburey, not out	5
Extras (b 2, lb 5, w 2, nb 9)	18
TOTAL (7 wkts)	261

R. G. D. Willis and M. Hendrick did not bat.

Fall of Wickets: 1–0, 2–18, 3–88, 4–101, 5–127, 6–144, 7–237.

Bowling: Lillee, 30–10–70–4; Alderman, 19–6–60–2; Whitney, 11–4–46–1; Bright, 27–12–50–0; Yallop, 8–2–17–0.

Match drawn.

Umpires: H. D. Bird and B. J. Meyer.

natural position. In the 'trial' match against Sri Lanka
in June only Larkins, Emburey told me, had looked in
Gatting's class. He had been a reserve for much of the
summer. Now that a vacancy had occurred at No. 1 it
seemed sensible to give him a chance, especially as a
stroke-maker was being left out. The selectors were also
keen to have a look at Paul Parker, who had done all that
could be asked of him at county level. I wondered if he
had corrected an earlier fault of playing seam-bowling
with a slightly crooked bat outside off-stump. He is a
marvellous fielder, in the class of Gower, Randall,
Butcher and Barlow, if not at the top of it.

We all collectively – and I particularly – found it hard to
know whom to leave out. One could never write Boycott
off; many had been tempted to do so during the 1978–9
tour of Australia, when he was depressed by personal
loss and by Yorkshire wranglings. Yet he had bounced
back. If we had to pick one person to play for our lives, it
would be Boycott, the ultimate batting survivor. What of
Gower and Gatting? Gower's first match after the West
Indies tour was for the MCC versus Middlesex at Lord's.
All his old looseness had gone; he went for balls outside
the off-stump only when they were short or over-
pitched. His defence was sure and watchful. He had
taken a great step forward, I thought, in the year since
I had seen him bat regularly during the Australian tour.
Even so, during the series some old weaknesses had re-
appeared. At Old Trafford he had again been deceived by
early bouncers from Alderman, and had played all too
freely outside his off-stump. Just as it is often hard to
decide whether to praise Botham for his boldness or
criticise him for his foolhardiness, to praise Boycott for
his self-discipline or blame him for his inhibitions, so
with Gower the question arises: is he casual or relaxed,
loose or brilliant? Mike Gatting was also hard to assess.
At best he is both pugnacious and sound, but at Old
Trafford he was still planting the left foot where the bat
should be; he also repeated errors against the bouncer.

He had had many opportunities, but his highest Test score remained only 59.

Such decisions can never be more than hunches. Oddly enough, Gatting's modest bowling helped him retain his place, now that the useful seam-bowling of Gooch and Woolmer would be lacking. Gower was the unlucky one.

As Old was now fit, we brought him back into the twelve, omitting Underwood, since the Oval pitch was likely to be fast and firm. Otherwise it was the same team as at Manchester. As usual it was left to me to phone those who had been left out. I was sad that it should be Gower and Gooch, the two most talented younger batsmen to emerge over the past five years, and both integral and well-liked members of the team that had come together while I was captain. I was authorised by the chairman to sweeten the pill by telling them that they were almost certain to go to India. I managed to contact Gower at Old Trafford during a break for rain on Saturday; but the only response at Northampton, where Gooch was playing for Essex, was a recorded message instructing members how to apply for tickets for the final of the National Westminster Cup. I finally contacted the Essex players' hotel later in the evening, only to be told that Gooch was not staying with the team. Ray East came on to the line; 'At last you've called me: I'll never let you down! How wonderful that you had confidence in me,' he said; then mentioned that in his only experience of my captaincy – in a jubilee match for the West Bengal Cricket Association at Calcutta in January 1981 – I had led the side to a 200-run defeat. I asked him to give Graham the message.

I omitted to tell Underwood, mainly because he had not played at Old Trafford. Also we had decided that if the pitch called for a second spinner he would be the one to be brought in. He had not, exactly, been dropped. I was not to know that only the batting changes would be announced over the loudspeaker during his Sunday league match at Folkestone, so that Derek accepted people's congratulations fully believing that he was in the twelve – until the tea interval, when his mother, who had seen the team-list on television, rang to commiserate.

On Wednesday the weather was set fair. Harry Brind, the groundsman, had prepared two pitches. One was a new strip, relaid less than two years before, and the other an old one as standby, likely to be slow and easy. The new pitch would be much quicker; the only doubt being whether the turfs would have knitted perfectly to give an even bounce. Harry was confident that this pitch would play well. It certainly looked promising; as Willis said, hard enough to be Perth rather than the Oval. It was also well-grassed. We had some minor anxiety over Botham's late arrival. Rumour had it that he had arranged a flying lesson that morning, and we scanned the sky for light aircraft, half expecting him to land on the outfield, a *deus ex machina*. The truth was less exotic. He had visited some children in hospital with leukaemia, and his message that he might be late had failed to reach me. He did have a puffy knee; so I was quite happy for him not to practise.

Old's fitness was once more in doubt, so Hendrick was also present. Poor Old! In all the Tests I played with him he always kept going well once he made it on to the field; but getting that far was rarely without problem. His knee was now fine; but during Yorkshire's last match he had ricked his back. He had a try-out in the afternoon. On the 'sporty' net pitches he ran in and bowled – even with an old ball – with splendidly aggressive panache for an hour, hitting both Gatting and me in the chest before clutching his back and retiring to the pavilion. I did not discover that the injury was irremediable (in the short term) until the team meeting that evening, from which Old was absent. With only a slightly different psychosomatic constitution, Chris Old could have been one of cricket's great players, instead of being merely an extremely good Test player.

The outcome of the series may have been settled, but hours before the start the Oval was ringed with queues of people hoping to get seats on the lovely late summer's day. Perhaps, I thought, this embodiment of fervour and support would prevent any complacency creeping into our play. Four years before, when we had also come to the Oval with an unassailable lead, our catching and fielding for the first time was ordinary. It was for his slip fielding as well as for his reliability as a bowler that we chose Hendrick rather than Allott.

The other critical decision facing us on the morning of the match was what to do if we won the toss. It would be hot later; but the morning haze suggested perfect conditions for swing bowling, and the pitch would be at its liveliest at the start of the match. Brind's opinion was that it would be easier for batting as the match went on, though the ball might keep low later. There was not much chance of the wicket taking spin. Botham wanted to bowl, but Willis thought otherwise. 'All I can say is, don't complain if it's cloudy when it's our turn to bat,' he said. I was torn. I asked Mickie Stewart, Surrey's manager, who knew the new pitches as well as anyone. 'I'd field first,' he said. 'These pitches last for a week or more without cracking up. There'll be more help for the bowlers early on, and the ball should swing.' At 10 o'clock, Jim Laker told Paul Parker's father that he thought we should field first. I would have happily lost this toss and left the decision to Hughes. I won it, and asked him to bat.

Australia had replaced Dyson with Dirk Wellham. The 22-year-old schoolmaster from Sydney had earned his first cap by scoring steadily against the counties. We knew him from 1979, when he had scored 95 for the Combined Universities against us at Adelaide. We were not unduly bothered by his selection; we knew that he liked to 'work' the ball to leg; so we reckoned to bowl straight to him at the start and later – on a good pitch –

just outside his off-stump. We also knew that he was an excellent fielder.

Kent opened the innings with Wood. The morning's play was fascinating, but frustrating. Wood hooked Willis high towards fine-leg; Larkins, Knott and I converged on the ball, which landed just out of the reach of us all. At Old Trafford, Kent had aimed to force anything short outside the off-stump, so I placed a man 40 or 50 yards from the bat at third man, hoping for a top edge; Emburey, in the gully, went squarer, also for the forcing shot. In the event, Kent played a more restrained innings throughout, and in Willis's second over the ball lobbed up off the shoulder of his defensive bat, landing between slips and gully, for what would have been a simple catch had we had an orthodox attacking field.

At the Oval, the Australian batting matured from the obsessive defence that had characterised much of their play in the third and fourth Tests, and the manic stroke-play of the fifth, to a more resolute, sensible approach. I sometimes found it hard to predict how some of their batsmen would set about their job. Boycott or Tavaré, Gooch or Botham, each has a consistent approach; not so Kent, Hughes or Yallop.

Possibly I made a mistake on the first morning in not opening with Botham. I knew that Willis and he would opt for all-out attack, whereas Hendrick with his impeccable length would neither waste the new ball nor be hit for too many runs. In the event, Hendrick seemed to have lost some of his 'nip' at the end of a long season. All our bowlers beat the bat from time to time; and Wood looked uncertain against the bouncer. In between, both batsmen played splendidly. I brought Emburey on early, since neither had been confident against him in earlier matches. Kent was obviously determined to remove me from silly mid-off, playing some wild strokes in the process. Emburey's field to him was deep square-leg, short square-leg, mid-wicket and mid-on; mid-off, extra-cover, deep square cover, slip and silly mid-off – an unusual field for an off-spinner aiming to bowl at middle-and-leg, but suitable for Kent as he so much favours the off-side.

A captain is always, illogically, criticised more sharply when the opposition score a large total after he has put them in than when his own side collapses when he bats first. In Friday's newspaper, Laker wrote that it was a mistake – facile criticism after the event. I had some unpleasant telegrams from an anonymous group calling themselves 'Brit barrackers beleaguered in Canberra'. When the score read 120 for no wicket, and the pitch was playing well, I began to wish that I had taken the other option myself. The truth is that in situations which are evenly balanced you can't tell whether the other route would have been more profitable. Lillee and Alderman would have found the conditions on Thursday morning much to their liking.

Thanks to Botham, the rest of the day turned out better for us. It was a Botham bouncer that caused Wood to change his mind about hooking, but fail to take his bat away; the result was a catch to me. 120–1 became 125–2 when Kent drove a half volley to mid-off, and after tea Hughes obligingly touched the stumps with his foot while pulling Botham to the boundary. The Australian captain gave a good imitation of innocent unawareness when the position of the leg-bail, lying on the ground behind the stumps, was pointed out to him. I was re-minded of Bill Lawry, who disturbed a bail while batting at Fenner's in 1968. He ran through for 2, but was given out. I asked him afterwards what he had thought before the decision. 'When I saw the bail lying on the ground,' he said, 'I thought the outlook wasn't too rosy.' Earlier, Botham had taken a superb one-handed catch high above his head to dismiss Yallop, who had again looked in excellent form; Willis was the bowler, and I had almost taken him off the previous over. Australia ended the day on 251–4, with a ball only three overs old ready for the next morning.

Our main anxiety on Friday was the state of our fast-bowlers. Hendrick was already suffering from a strained rib muscle sustained during the first afternoon. At first he thought it was a stitch; but he was unable to bowl flat out for the rest of the match. Worse was to come. Overnight Botham had trapped a nerve in his back and could hardly get his socks on. He said he would be all right if he bowled at medium pace. We allowed the press to believe that he had intentionally cut down on his pace to allow the ball to swing. Later that morning Willis too broke down after a hostile new ball spell: he had pulled stomach muscles. I suppose we had been fortunate in the resilience of our four-man bowling attack throughout the summer. Certainly having three injuries in twenty-four hours underlined the risk of this selection policy.

Nevertheless, our depleted attack gave one of its best performances in taking the remaining six Australian wickets for 101 runs, 32 of them for the last wicket. Willis and Botham took three wickets each. Overall, we had not done badly, catching all the chances offered. Parker's fielding was marvellous; his nerves must have been eased by being able to revel in his fielding. For Australia, Border again was their bulwark. Such trouble as he had came from Botham's swing, but in the main he carried on where he had left off at Manchester, and once again shielded Whitney from most of the bowling. Botham, annoyed by the somewhat comical determination of the young fast-bowler, bowled him a couple of near-bouncers, and was not unduly perturbed by the batsman's intimation of retaliation. Umpire Bird became fretful at this turn of events, but everyone else took it more lightly. I could see nothing wrong in bouncing Whitney, who is one of those irritating tail-enders who stop the straight balls and miss the wide ones. He had kept Border company to his 100 (and for over an hour in their two consecutive Test partnerships) and when at last he edged Botham for his first Test runs his overt pleasure at this feat surpassed even Border's at his century.

In reply to Australia's 352, Boycott and Larkins opened our innings at 2.40. Larkins played very well, driving Lillee crisply wide of mid-on and forcing him on the off-side off the back foot. Lillee was given the choice of ends, with the wind coming from mid-on; but in the early stages Alderman looked the more dangerous. Larkins was well set when he played loosely at Lillee and was caught at slip. His dismissal made the score 61–1. Tavaré – the hero or the villain of Old Trafford – again incurred the wrath of the more voluble sections of the crowd. But in the three hours, until the close, our total reached 100–1. We were happy with the day's work.

That evening I talked to Hughes about his opening bowlers. He told me that Alderman had taken even his team-mates by surprise on the tour by bowling much faster than at home, without losing accuracy or movement. Today Kim would have liked to have given Alderman choice of ends with the new ball – Lillee's direction had been wasteful. Perhaps it was only his reputation that earned Lillee the preference.

Next day the senior bowler in effect answered any such unspoken criticism. For the remainder of the match he once again bowled at his best. It was a classic encounter, Lillee v. Boycott, on a good cricket pitch; by which I mean one with enough bounce and pace to help the best bowlers, but also fairly true. In a single spell Lillee hit Boycott on the helmet, jaw and shoulder; yet his bowling was never primarily intimidatory, but full of skilful variation. It is in these conditions, too, that Boycott's skill is best displayed, rather than on slow pitches against less penetrative bowlers, where his control can become mechanical. He had had his luckiest moment on the second evening, when Alderman dropped a sharp low chance at slip off Whitney. Otherwise he played extremely well to reach his seventh Test century against Australia. In the same innings, Lillee had his best-ever Test bowling figures, 7–89, his previous best being 6–26 in the Centenary Test at Melbourne. The cricket, like the season, suggested a mellow fruitfulness.

As Willis had gloomily predicted, Saturday morning was overcast. However, we lost only one wicket before 3 o'clock, that of Tavaré, who was caught behind attempting to repeat a square-cut off one of Lillee's less taxing deliveries. Gatting came in at 131–2 to play at his best; he and Boycott added 115 before Hughes took the new ball, a few overs after it became due.

Just at this point the sun came out – and from then on our innings fell apart. Gatting, on 53, let the first delivery with the new ball go; it did not deviate, to hit off-stump. I tried to take my bat away from Alderman, the ball came back and took the edge, while the débutant, Parker, hung his bat out to be caught in the slips in the same over. 246–2 had become 248–5. Worse followed, for 10 runs later Botham was again caught in the gully.

Meanwhile Wood had dropped yet another chance at first slip, giving Boycott a life off Lillee when he had scored 121. This escape seemed likely to be crucial as Boycott and Knott added 37 runs for the seventh wicket, but Lillee gained his deserts by having his main antagonist brilliantly caught by Yallop in the gully for 137. It had been a contest of rare vintage. The tail folded rapidly, though not without some outrageous improvisations by Knott who was last out for 36. Our innings, which had been developing so promisingly, totalled a disappointing 314, a deficit of 38. In the last hour, however, a wicket each to Botham and Hendrick for 36 runs· allowed us to enjoy the prospect of the rest-day from a more comfortable vantage-point. If only a day off would miraculously cure our ailing attack! 'Bustling Bob', as the Australians had named Willis, was reduced to bowling at little more than half-pace. Hogg had a name for me which he'd been using without explanation for a few days – MTA. He now told me it stood for Mike The Athlete. One of the advantages of cricket over most other sports is that it accommodates such a range of shapes and sizes, weights and ages. Quentin's own body continued to let him down. He had bowled a very fast spell, by all accounts, at Hove just before the Test, provoked by his dismissal with a catch that he claimed was taken on the half-volley. But by the end of it his back was again troubling him. Unkindly, I suggested to him that he turned in these aggressive spells against the counties just frequently enough not to be sent home. I gather that there really was a trace of this suspicion among his senior team-mates. We who had faced him at his best when in 1978–9 he broke the record for wickets taken by an Australian in a series against England perhaps had a healthier respect for his bowling than some of his colleagues, who had missed that series because of Packer. Certainly any suspicion of malingering was dispelled when two months later the crack in his vertebrae was discovered.

On Monday morning our bowlers had not recovered; but the team fought tenaciously, Hendrick dismissing Wood early on and Yallop at 12.25. Australia were now 105–4, a position we could not, in the circumstances, have hoped for. We had rarely looked like getting wickets in entirely orthodox ways, so I had switched the bowling frequently, and placed unusual fields to try to unsettle the batsmen; silly mid-off, for example, to Border when Willis or Botham was bowling, and short mid-wicket to him for Botham in the hope that he might misdrive an in-swinger. While I was fielding at silly mid-off, Border gave me an indication of the high standards he set himself: he drove Willis past cover for 2, but when he came back to take strike he was muttering to himself under his breath. 'Bad shot, bad shot. Too wide. Concentrate.'

Botham was swinging the ball a lot, if at a gentle pace, and he almost bowled the left-hander with a full-toss, then nearly had him caught at mid-on. For the most part, though, Border was ominously sound. Our big chance came shortly before lunch when Wellham, trying to drive Botham through mid-wicket, offered a simple chance to

Willis at mid-on. Willis missed the catch, and we, as it turned out, had missed the boat.

After lunch, I think I made a mistake in going on the defensive too soon. Defensive field placing is at times necessary, provided always that bowlers and captain are still purposive and probing. We allowed things to slide, and for once accepted as inevitable what was only likely. It was, at last, a change of plan that gained us a wicket. Border, who like Yallop is a superb player of spin, had been scoring freely on the off-side against Emburey. John suggested going over the wicket to him, and bowling at his leg-stump. Out of the blue he made one turn sharply from that line, finding the edge as Border tried to play the ball to mid-wicket, and Tavaré took a good catch to his right at slip.

At 205–5, we still might have bowled Australia out for, say, 250, and had a feasible target. But the wicket was easy, Willis was finally off the field for good, and Botham and Hendrick were at last tiring. Even Knott was below his best, failing to gather an awkward low throw from Emburey that would have run Marsh out by yards, and missing his opposite number when he edged an attempted pull off Botham. It was during this match that I discovered why Knott fastens his pads unconventionally, with a broad strip of sticky-tape in place of the middle strap and buckle. He once saw the New Zealand wicket-keeper, Ken Wadsworth, struck on the inside of the knee by a throw-in that dropped short; his pad had swivelled round and left his knee unprotected. The injury forced him to miss the next match. Knott took this as a caution, and figured out a method of avoiding similar risk. With his pads secured to his trousers it is impossible for them to skew round. He also finds that the tape avoids chafing. I admire the professionalism of a man who is prepared to dress oddly if not ridiculously for a slight though definite gain.

Whatever England's shortcomings, the day belonged to Wellham. In the first innings Willis's steep bounce had caused him a lot of trouble. Softened up, he had missed a straight ball of fuller length. Now, with no one able to threaten his ribs, he looked more comfortable. He favours the on-side – Botham never lost hope of trapping him LBW, attempting to work a straight ball towards mid-wicket – but he also drove well on the off-side. He leans back too much for the purist, so that there is a tendency for the ball to go in the air. However, he watched the ball carefully, and played with increasing confidence until he became stuck on 99. When he arrived there Hughes must have been keen on an immediate declaration: Australia were almost 370 runs ahead, and we would have had an awkward half hour on the Monday evening. Boycott himself contributed to our avoiding this little ordeal by dropping Wellham off Hendrick at mid-off. Then Bright was out; appropriately, as by this time dark clouds were gathering. Hughes sent a message via Lillee, the next batsman, to the effect that no declaration would be made before close, so Wellham could take his time. Botham beat him outside the off-stump and sat him on the ground with a bouncer. Typically, he also had time to tell the young batsman not to throw it away. Finally, after 25 agonising minutes, Wellham drove him through extra-cover to complete a gritty century.

I would not have given a batsman as much leeway as Hughes did. I think a deadline of, say, 5.20 was called for, and if he had not reached his 100 by then I would have declared to allow our opening bowlers half an hour at the opposition. However, sentiment is part of the game, and it would have been excruciating to deny someone his century when he had come so close.

The delay was doubly unfortunate. For at this stage in the series I should have been prepared to instruct our batsmen to go hard for a target if I felt we had even a modest chance of reaching it. When a series is still undecided, it is reasonable for the captain of the side batting last to calculate the odds carefully before risking defeat. But in this Test I could afford to be magnanimous.

Similarly, at tea time in the famous Centenary Test at Melbourne I urged Greig to go flat out for a win even if the odds were 5–1 against us. We had already done fantastically well to come close to the enormous target of 465 in the last innings. My advice would have been different if it had been an early match in a long campaign.

On Monday evening I toyed with the idea of chasing 383 in five hours plus twenty overs, but by the clear light of the following morning realised that scoring over 4 runs an over for an entire day was out of the question. Apart from all else, Botham was exhausted; anyway, it was undesirable both for him and for the other batsmen to pin one's hopes on one man too often. So the instructions were for each batsman to play the way that suited himself.

The biggest blow came in the very first over, when Lillee brought a ball back to have Boycott palpably LBW. Tavaré followed 45 minutes later; he edged Whitney – bowling quite fast – to first slip, where Kent took the first of three excellent catches. Gatting played a splendid innings, full of confident hooks and drives, and though Larkins struggled at times he lasted until shortly after lunch when Lillee made one bounce and move away: beautiful bowling. Parker escaped a 'pair' with a snick past leg-stump off Lillee. Having started my Test career with a duck, I feared ending it with another. *Private Eye* had once suggested that my favourite piece of music was Haydn's Duck Quartet; I should then have been able to call this book 'Full Circle'. With more than usual relief I nudged a single to square-leg.

Australia's tactics were sensible enough. They used the quick bowlers at the Pavilion End, while Bright wheeled away at the Vauxhall End. The ball was turning more now, and the bounce was a little irregular. Besides, they needed to bowl their overs quickly in order to allow themselves a reasonable ration of overs with the second new ball. When Parker was out at 127–5, Botham had to be woken to come in to bat. He looked sleepy as he ran his first ball through gully for 3, then played as if he intended either to knock the runs off by teatime or get back to his snooze. After ten eventful minutes in which poor Whitney was again tested with a steepling half-chance running back from mid-off, Botham pulled at a good length ball from Alderman and was LBW for 16. Thus Alderman took his 42nd wicket of the series and beat Hogg's record.

With only four wickets in hand we still had to survive for an hour and forty minutes plus twenty overs. It was of course very satisfying for me to play a worthwhile innings in my last Test, and enjoyable to have the company of Knott for most of it. His method of saving the game was unusual, to say the least. While Bright kept close fielders, he swept virtually every ball – and never missed. The secret, he says, is to get as low as possible, keep one's head still and the bat parallel to the ground, and avoid the temptation to hit too hard. It is remarkable how even ordinary players, if they set their minds to Knott's technique, rarely miss the ball. Against the seamers he played some remarkable off-drives and slashes with minimal movement of the feet. This method is not so easily imitated. Even Knott tried to stop himself from playing at balls outside the off-stump, but like the umpire who once apologised for giving me out, caught off my pad-strap, with the words, 'I felt my arm going up and couldn't stop it,' he just couldn't control himself.

With twelve overs to go, I was out to Lillee. Emburey and Knott had to face ten overs with the second new ball. They decided each to take one end, Knott facing Alderman, Emburey Lillee. Alderman looked justifiably tired; Lillee forced himself to effort after effort. With three overs to go, he had Emburey dropped by the usually safe Border in the slips. Even in the last over he cut one back at high speed to go over Emburey's stumps; but no further wickets fell. Fred Bennett could have had little hesitation in making Dennis Lillee man of the match for his eleven wickets, and Alec Bedser even less in naming Ian Botham man of the series.

10

Of Beer and Breweries

Post-natal depression is common for mothers, and students often have a similar experience after exams. There is also, I find, a post-Test and post-series let-down – even when you win.

Anticlimax hits me immediately after a match, or earlier if the conclusion has long been foregone, so it is not easy to respond with the excitement that is expected in the television and radio interviews that follow hard on the now customary award ceremony. I can understand Bob Willis's feeling less than euphoric after his inspired spell at Headingley, for instance, when he annoyed some viewers with his caustic comments about the press. His entire physical and mental energy had been pressed into a nugget of single-mindedness; when other thoughts were allowed in, it is not surprising that dammed-up feelings of resentment at being written off, personally and as a team, came flooding out.

The interviews are, of course, a regular part of the captain's job. Meanwhile, the players, glum or glad, shower, pack, sip champagne from the glass, or lager from the can. After nearly a week of conflict and in-jokes, of exhausting work and exacting co-operation, the unit mustered at the selectors' whim but created (in its character) by its members dismantles. The haphazard order of the dressing room, the sprawling gear and hazy territories, of TV and fruit and autographs, gives way to the littered disorder of wet towels, last bats to be signed, laundry wrappers and discarded hangers.

By the time I got back to the dressing-room, half the players would have left, for Scarborough or Taunton,

Leicester or Hove. Relationships within the side would never be the same again. Loss, then, is involved in both winning and losing, but easier to put up with for the winners. I wouldn't have enjoyed my return to Test Cricket if we had lost every match! How then did we end up on top, albeit so narrowly?

The main factor was the return to form of both Botham and Willis. Enough has been written about Ian, but for half the Leeds Test right through to his injury on the second day at The Oval, Bob's transformation was equally crucial. For that time, Willis was the only really quick bowler on either side. He alone could, on slowish pitches, regularly force batsmen on to the back foot, and pepper their fingers. Most batsmen are happier when they can 'come to' the ball, rather than when they have to play high up off the back foot. (An exception is Bruce Laird, the gritty Western Australian who has played so well against the West Indies.) Hughes, Yallop and, to a lesser extent, Border are twice as dangerous when they can get into a rhythm of forward play.

Willis's previous three series had been frustrating. By the third Test in Australia in 1979–80, his body had refused to function for him, and his movements became staccato and dislocated. In the summer of 1980, he bowled well for two Tests against West Indies, but in the third looked past it; and the following winter he had to fly home from the Caribbean for a new operation before the Tests had begun. So it was a colossal physical and mental achievement not only to make his way back to the top but also to bowl faster and better as the series went on.

Botham's bowling also was reinvigorated. The two of them, with invaluable support from others, but especially from Old and Emburey, gave the new thrust to our out-cricket. Certainly the most enjoyable times for me as captain were the fielding sessions when we bowled Australia at Leeds, Birmingham and Manchester.

It was a series in which class and experience counted for a lot. Boycott struggled through on the awkward pitches, always bearing the brunt of Lillee and Alderman at their freshest. After his failures at Birmingham, he was anxious and in need of reassurance. At last he fought through to calmer waters at the Oval, and against a Lillee bowling better than at any time during the summer.

Perhaps Lillee was only then fully recovered from his serious illness. At the Oval he bowled pretty quickly; he swung the ball out and in late enough for it not to be clear whether the movement was in the air or off the pitch. He varied his pace, and bowled some slower, deceptive leg-cutters. He kept going to the very end. Has there ever been a bowler to equal him?

Like Taylor and Knott, Marsh had a fine series behind the stumps. I have a great affection and regard for Hughes, but I'm surprised that Australia have never made Marsh captain. Tactically, he made many shrewd suggestions; publicly combative and privately warm, Marsh has always struck me as a man whom most cricketers would follow with a will.

Australia were unlucky with the weather early on; and with injuries to Lawson and Hogg. Somehow, Hogg never quite seems to be rated highly enough by the current hierarchy of players, never made to feel important. He can, without question, be a superb fast bowler. However, their disappointments over Hogg and Lawson were for the most part compensated for by the colossal impact of Alderman, playing in his first Test series, and breaking Hogg's own record.

I cannot mention all those who made important contributions for Australia; but, of their batsmen, Border most gave an impression of impregnability on a decent pitch. He is a correct and complete player who would have done even better if he had been able to bat at five or six all through. He rarely plays at wide balls unless he is certain he can cut or drive with safety. He commits himself late to his shot. He is also a brilliant player of spin bowling, as is Yallop, and it is much to Emburey's credit that he dismissed Border twice, and Yallop three times, in the series.

For Kim Hughes, 1981 must have been a desperately frustrating season. With just ordinary luck at Heading-ley, his team would have won comfortably. Probably there would have been no revival by England after that (though as a country we have specialized in doing badly at the beginning of wars and ending up victorious!). Hughes would have earned unmitigated applause for his energy, verve and friendliness, as well as for his obvious ability to weld Australia into a powerful force. Instead, he came up against Botham in his glory, whose impact would have thrown any captain's tactics into confusion. Not surprisingly, there were moments when Hughes seemed uncertain which way to turn. It would be odd, too, if a modicum of the frustration felt by Marsh and Lillee – two of the giants of cricket – did not on occasion find an outlet in scapegoating their younger captain. Out of this situation Hughes emerged with credit. He remained robust and straightforward. He concentrated absolutely. He acknowledged his side's lapses without ever running them down, or 'wingeing' about their luck. He was an excellent representative for his country, and won many admirers.

No doubt he was not sorry to hand the captaincy back to Greg Chappell for the home series against Pakistan and West Indies, in which Australia did well, winning 2–1 against the former and drawing 1–1 with West Indies. The intensity of their programme, though, which included a three-Test series in New Zealand in February and March, underlined Hughes's plea for less international cricket.

England, too, had an exacting winter ahead – though the issue of South Africa came close to causing their seven-Test tour of India and Sri Lanka to be cancelled. Widely divergent interpretations of the Gleneagles Agreement – which pledged the signatories 'vigorously to combat the evil of apartheid' in the field of sport – led to a dangerous impasse. Despite the narrow escape for this particular tour, it was already likely that the differing

TIMES

MONDAY AUGUST 17 1981

Price twenty pence

DIEU ET MON DROIT

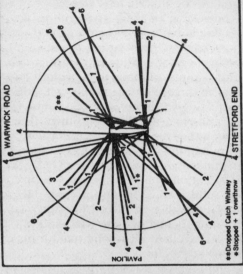

WARWICK ROAD

PAVILION

STRETFORD END

**Dropped Catch Whitney
*Stopped + 1 overthrow

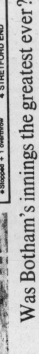

Was Botham's innings the greatest ever?

attitudes of white and non-white cricketing countries
would result in cancellations and schisms in the future,
especially at a time when extremely lucrative offers from
South Africa were being dangled in front of international
players.

The controversy had raised its head during the season,
in connection with proposed unofficial tours of South
Africa, as well as with the black-listing of Boycott
and other contenders for tour places by a United
Nations committee. At Birmingham, for example, I was
approached by Edrich; he asked if I would consider
captaining a near-Test team to tour South Africa in the
autumn. I could, I gathered, have virtually named my
price. Many other players were similarly sounded
out. My answer was no. Despite recognising that the
cricketers of that country have done virtually all they can
to make the game multi-racial, I have no inclination to
play cricket in South Africa. In my view, it is only by the
ban on international sport with that country that these
desirable changes have taken place. And despite the
apparent injustice in sportsmen being almost alone in
bearing the brunt of the protests against South Africa my
view is that the evil of that system and the opportunity
that sportsmen have to dent it outweigh such con-
siderations.

In October 1981 the tour of India, due to begin on
5 November, seemed certain to be cancelled. The Indian
government had banned Boycott and Cook, and the
TCCB had replied that they were not willing to change
their team. The ban was eventually withdrawn a week or
so before the players flew to Bombay. Though the major

Botham's century inspired *The Times* to a front page article,
possibly the first time any cricketing innings had been awarded
such treatment in 'The Thunderer'. The article was written by
John Woodcock who commented that Botham had showed
himself 'able to scale heights beyond the reach of ordinary
men'. The chart of the innings is by Wendy Wimbush.

reason for Mrs Gandhi's relenting must have been political expediency, other factors may have helped. The TCCB had on 4 August sent letters to many leading players warning us that 'any cricketer who takes part in any such International and/or representative match in South Africa could, thereby, make himself ineligible for future selection for England'. And a sentence in one of Boycott's books, in which he expressed his own opposition to apartheid, may have influenced the outcome.

Mrs Gandhi would not have been the only one to raise a sardonic eyebrow when the news broke on 28 February 1982 that Boycott and other leading English cricketers had landed in South Africa for a tour which had been secretly planned and organised since before the England team arrived in India. The Indians were not the only people to be kept in the dark. Raman Subba Row, the tour manager, and Keith Fletcher, the captain, were kept in ignorance of meetings held throughout the tour by an inner cabal of players. The enterprise thus resembled the Packer 'revolution' of 1977 not only in being a threat to Test cricket – and therefore to county cricket and the incomes of their fellow-cricketers – but also in the shabbiness and deceit of its conception and birth.

With predictable banality, the spokesmen of the players claimed that they were in South Africa simply to play cricket. And as if to refute the idea that it was a purely business, i.e. cricketing visit, the South Africans, laughably, awarded springbok caps for those picked to play against this motley crew of Englishmen assembled under the flag of the South African Breweries Company. If Mrs Gandhi was indeed swayed by the sentence in Boycott's book, I doubt if she or other government leaders would be likely to be influenced again by the personal disclaimers of sportsmen who choose to play in South Africa.

The actual tour of India, hailed at the start as a triumph for commonsense, was a dull affair, overshadowed in

A cartoonist's view of Boycott. A complicated, convoluted character, he was almost always a helpful source of sound ideas for me, both before and during Tests. Our rare tiffs were more widely publicized.

retrospect by the political events surrounding and running through it. England were involved in a long struggle on slow wickets to try to force a win after losing the first Test in Bombay. Against Australia in 1981, the over-rate of both sides was around 14 per hour, but this was lost sight of since the cricket was so tense. In India, the rate was even slower, only 12 overs being bowled each hour. Perhaps one positive result of the tour will be that other countries besides England will be prepared to take steps to force the over-rate back up. I favour fines (a method that we operated with some success in the home series in 1978 and 1979, but only on our own players) and a minimum number of overs each day. This latter method was turned down by Australia in 1981.

There was a strange coincidence of achievement in the winter of 1981–2 by two of the great protagonists of England v. Australia cricket. Within a few weeks of each other Lillee and Boycott broke, respectively, the records for wickets and runs in Test cricket.

As for me, the summer of 1981 was an extraordinary climax to a cricket career in which playing for England at all had been an unexpected bonus. For I was already 34 when I was first picked for a Test match, against West Indies at Trent Bridge in 1976. Needless to say, I enjoyed this final icing on the cake enormously. The worst time was when I was convinced of the selection mistake for which I alone was responsible – when we left Emburey out at Headingley. I rarely feel bad about decisions that have unsuccessful consequences. Putting Australia in to bat at the Oval did not work too well; but I would probably repeat the decision in the same situation. I still cringe at not placing a short-leg for Kent's first ball in Test cricket – that decision I *would* reverse if I had the chance!

The most vivid memories – apart from memories of Botham – are of the drama of the last days' play at Headingley and Edgbaston. Such excitement of co-ordinated team activity is rare in sport at any level. Yet a cricket team is one of the heirs of the primitive hunting band, and the pleasures of mutual help, of a campaign that results in the climax of a kill, of planning that comes right and of supreme effort from all, are deep, almost instinctual sources of human satisfaction. And when everything falls into place on the large canvas of a Test series against Australia, the excitement is even more intense.

None of this could have happened without one man, Ian Botham. 'I QUIT', blared the placards on 8 July. A mere 13 days later he was the hero of the land. Luck played some part – bad luck before and good luck after. But without doubt, and whatever Botham's view may be, it was a relief to him to be captain no longer. And no doubt at that moment of depression if not humiliation it was easier for Ian to accept me as his replacement than anyone else. For I was in no sense a rival, and my re-appointment was not the snub that might have come his way. His tremendous performances against Australia were not an isolated feat. He also played with massive authority and maturity in India. As a player there is no limit to what he is capable of achieving.

But what of Botham the captain? Will, or should, the selectors ever again appoint Ian Botham captain of England? Predictions and judgements are notoriously hard to make in cricket. Let me prove this point by quoting two excellent judges of a cricketer, Greg Chappell and Ray Illingworth. Both were writing shortly after the Lord's Test. Chappell said: 'Botham will never be the same force again. When you're young you just race out and do it.' Illingworth was even more categorical. 'Botham is not the player he was . . . He may not be seen for two seasons at the top level. His form does not warrant a place in the England team.'

Botham gloriously proved them wrong, and he will probably do the same for me if I were to predict that he will not captain his country again. What I am prepared to say is, that to appoint him to that position again would be to run the risk of reducing the greatest English cricketer since W. G. Grace from genius to mediocrity.

Index

Adelaide 18, 77, 161

Age (Melbourne) 35

Ahmedabad 15

Alderly Edge 121

Alderman, Terry 13–14, 19–20, 26–8, 56, 71, 73–5, 79–81, 98–102, 106, 110–11, 117, 140–2, 145–7, 153, 158, 163, 165–6, 171, 174

Allen, G. O. B. 8

Allott, Paul 137, 142–4, 150–4, 161

Allsop, Ron 9, 78

Arlott, John 41

Ashes, the 33, 36, 55, 90, 121, 127, 154–5

Asif Iqbal 129, 132

Athey, Bill 16

Australian Cricket Board 36

Bangalore 133

Bangladesh 126

Barclay, John 5

Barlow, Graham 21, 44, 47, 158

Barrington, Ken 6, 38–40, 51

Basingstoke 47

Bath 136

Beard, Graham 137

Bedfordshire 125

Bedser, Alec 1, 30, 33, 45, 51–2, 54, 62, 121, 136, 151, 155, 171

Benaud, Richie 108

Bennett, Fred 58, 171

Benson and Hedges Trophy 42

Bird, H. D. (Dicky) 100, 103–5, 164

Birmingham *see* Edgbaston

Bombay 3–5, 59, 177, 180

Border, Alan 12–14, 16, 28–9, 55, 59, 89, 102, 108, 112, 114–16, 144, 152–4, 164, 167–8, 171, 173–4

Botham, Ian:
  advice to Boycott, Geoffrey 4
  batting failure 3, 5–6, 26, 29, 59, 141, 170–1
  batting success 2–5, 75–7, 79, 81, 101, 146–9
  bowling failure 5–6, 59
  bowling success 3, 13, 28, 52, 69, 71, 73, 79, 86, 103, 116–17, 144–5, 151, 153, 163, 166, 173
  Brearley, Mike 1–8, 15–16, 28, 47–8, 55–6, 73, 75–6, 81–8, 97, 101, 103, 115–117, 122, 124, 138, 143–9, 151–3, 158, 173, 180–1
  captaincy 1–9, 15–16, 26, 29–30, 32, 48, 51, 97, 122, 180–1
  celebration 84
  character 2–8, 16, 29–30, 84, 103, 116–17, 145, 153, 158, 169
  criticism 6, 29–30, 146
  crowd 7, 117, 152
  diffidence 116
  encouragement 7
  exhaustion 168
  family 7, 8
  fast scoring 2–3, 75–83, 86, 146–9, 170–1
  fielding 7, 13, 14, 72, 88, 105, 116, 144, 152, 163
  fines 56
  form 5–6, 14, 55, 59, 97, 173
  friendship 7
  generosity 3, 169
  glory 175
  habits 6–7, 113, 123–4, 160, 170–1

Botham, Ian (continued)
  heroism 5, 71, 84, 180–1
  humour 2–3, 12, 16, 55, 75, 81, 84, 97, 109–10, 145–9, 151–2
  injury 5, 69, 164
  man of the match 133–4
  man of the series 171
  media 6–7, 16, 29–30, 84, 97, 164
  nicknames 145
  publicity 7, 84, 97
  stubbornness 6, 16, 116, 153, 163–4
  tactics 2–4, 16, 28–30, 60–3, 69, 71, 74–80, 84–7, 98, 116–17, 138, 144–7, 152, 163–4, 169–70
  technique 71–3, 75–6, 145–7, 163–4
  weight 6
  as all-rounder 3, 113, 180–1
  for England 1–16, 28–30, 52–6, 59–60, 68–87, 97–101, 103–5, 109, 113, 115–17, 133, 135, 138–41, 144–54, 158, 162–4, 166–71, 173
  nothing goes right for 6–8, 14–16
Botham, Mrs Ian 7, 84
Botham, Liam 84
Botham family 7, 84
Boyce, Keith 56
Boycott, Geoffrey 4, 13, 23, 26, 29, 33–5, 38, 41, 50, 53, 55, 59, 61–5, 70, 73–5, 79–80, 94–5, 97, 99, 106–11, 124, 132, 136, 138–40, 145–7, 154, 158, 162, 165–6, 169–70, 173, 177–9
Bradford 79
Brearley, H. 54
Brearley, Mike
  apartheid 175, 177–8
  Australians 9, 18–19, 22, 58, 60–1, 83–4, 88–9, 98, 127, 138, 162, 169, 171
  awarded OBE 41
  batting 21–2, 33, 38, 41, 44–7,

50, 52, 73–5, 77–80, 99–100, 106–7, 140–1, 146, 166, 170–1
  behaviour 41–3, 58, 61, 80
  Botham 1–6, 8–9, 16, 48, 51, 55, 71, 75, 79, 84, 86, 97, 116, 145, 151, 181
  captaincy 1–2, 6, 16, 22, 31–3, 35, 38, 40–7, 51, 63–5, 68, 72, 77, 80, 85, 95, 132, 138–9, 151, 155, 163, 169, 172, 177, 181
  character 5, 33, 35, 37
  coaching 39–40
  controlled aggression 41
  correspondence 118, 120–6
  criticism 38–9, 44, 72, 108–9, 149
  crowd 33, 35, 37, 41, 78
  discipline 38, 56, 97, 180
  dropping of 136
  exhaustion 47, 112
  family 31, 54, 113
  fielding 72–3, 85, 114, 153, 162–3
  friendship 31, 42, 51, 79, 90, 127–8
  groundsmen 12, 56, 78, 95
  injury 109
  Lillee's shirts 57–9, 61, 96
  media 47–50, 57–8, 71, 78, 80, 84, 95–7, 109, 172
  Middlesex 1, 9, 12, 18–19, 22, 40–1, 48, 60
  nickname 166
  Packer 35–7
  practice 38, 43, 49, 56–7, 62–3, 85, 95, 107, 137, 145–6
  psychoanalysis 1, 40, 45–7
  publicity 35, 96
  reporting 12, 35, 78
  selectors 1, 50–4, 64, 94, 129–39, 155, 158–60, 180
  sponsors 112–13
  tactics 63, 65, 68, 70–3, 76–7, 85–90, 102–4, 109, 113–14, 116, 139, 144, 147, 152–3, 161–2, 167–70, 180
  team 38–41, 45–6, 48–9, 86,

94–8, 106, 180–1
  technique 22, 40, 52
  Test Match record 180
  umpires 77, 86, 104
Brearley, Walter 121
Bright, Ray 9, 17, 22, 26, 28–9, 50,
    61, 72, 83, 87, 89–90, 99,
    101–3, 108–13, 116, 134, 141,
    144, 146, 152–3, 169–71
Brind, Harry 160–1
Brisbane 19, 133
British Broadcasting Corporation
  8
Brixton riots 119
Broadstairs 123
Burridge, Alan 32
Butcher, Alan 39
Butcher, Roland 16, 20, 42, 56, 158

Calcutta 159
Cambridge University 147
Canberra 163
Capes, Geoff 125
Cardiff 123
Carey, Michael 111
Carr, Donald 57–8
Carreras, Miranda 126
Centenary Test matches:
  Lord's 6, 15
  Melbourne 1, 74, 165–6
Chappell, Greg 3, 6, 19, 23, 35,
    105, 129, 137, 175, 181
Chappell, Ian 44, 129
Chappell, Trevor 23, 29, 60, 69–
    70, 87, 98, 102, 142
Charles, Prince of Wales 91
Cheltenham 137
Cleese, John 53
Close, Brian 51, 56, 75, 110–11,
  136
Collingwood, R. C. 49
Combined Universities 4, 161
Constant, David 131
Cook, Geoff 155, 177
Cornhill Insurance Company 112:
  see Test Matches
Cowdrey, Colin 59, 139

Cricket Revolution, The 39
Croft, Colin 18, 73

Daily Express 31, 42
Daily Mail 96
Daniel Wayne 18, 23, 42, 44, 73
Denness, Mike 2
Derby 94
Derbyshire CCC 5
Dilley, Graham 12, 14–16, 28–9,
    39, 52, 57, 59, 64, 68–9, 71–3,
    79–81, 83, 86, 89, 94, 123, 136
Doncaster 110
Downton, Paul 10, 16, 23, 31, 44
Durham University 18
Dymock, Geoff 19
Dyson, John 22, 60, 68–71, 75, 80,
    87–9, 97, 102–3, 112–13, 127,
    143, 150, 161

East, Ray 159
Edgbaston (Birmingham) 32, 46,
    52, 94, 97, 109, 112, 120,
    122–4, 127, 129, 132, 134, 136,
    146–7, 152, 173–4, 177, 180
Edge Hill 120
Edmonds, Phil 18, 42, 94
Edrich, John 56, 136, 177
Elliott, Charlie 1, 51, 64
Emburey, John 12, 23, 26–9, 42–3,
    48, 52–3, 57, 60, 64–5, 68, 87,
    101–3, 105–6, 110–11, 113–
    17, 129, 133, 142, 144, 150,
    152–4, 158, 162, 168, 171,
    173–4, 180
Essex CCC 12, 159
Evans, David 65, 83, 89

Fearnley, Duncan 48, 50, 81
Fenner's 163
Flack, Bernard 94
Fletcher, Keith 32, 90, 178
Folkestone 2, 160
Francis, Tony 97
Fry, C. B. 121

Gandhi, Mrs Indira 178
Garner, Joel 7, 73
Gatting, Mike 12–13, 15, 23, 26, 28, 42, 48, 53, 55, 59, 63, 69, 75, 78, 80, 85, 89–90, 100, 104, 106, 110, .112–13, 134, 136, 138, 141, 146, 150–1, 154, 158–60, 166, 170
Gavaskar, Sunil 149
Gifford, Norman 108
Gleneagles Agreement 175
Gloucestershire CCC 137
Golden Jubilee Test match 3
Gooch, Graham 13, 26, 28, 49–50, 53, 63–4, 71–3, 77, 79, 81, 85, 88, 94, 99–100, 106, 108–9, 123–4, 134, 136, 140, 144–5, 155, 159, 162
'Goose' *see* Willis, Bob
'Gorilla' *see* Botham, Ian
Gower, David 3, 13, 15–16, 26, 29, 39, 53, 56, 59, 70, 75, 80, 85, 94, 99, 103–8, 110, 124, 134, 136, 138, 140, 144, 146, 150, 154, 158–9
Grace, Dr W. G. 181
Greig, Tony 5, 37, 51, 170
Guardian 123

Hadlee, Richard 4, 137
Hall, Wesley 147
Hampshire CCC 137
Harrogate 78, 90
Harvey, Neil 88
Hawke, Bob 37
Hawkins, Chris 139
Headingley (Leeds) 1, 27, 33, 48, 52, 55–8, 61, 63–4, 71, 75, 77–8, 91, 95–7, 112–13, 117, 119–20, 123, 126, 132, 143, 146, 172, 175, 180
Hemmings, Eddie 53
Hendrick, Mike 13, 16, 23, 49, 53, 94–5, 160–2, 164, 166–9
Higgs, Jim 17
Hogg, Rodney 9, 22–3, 31, 61, 64, 79, 84, 99, 102, 106–7, 117,

137, 166, 174
Holding, Michael 7, 73
Holmes, Larry 125
Hove 41, 167, 173
Hughes, Kim 12, 18, 20–3, 28–9, 58–60, 62, 64, 68, 70–2, 77, 79–80, 83, 86, 88, 91, 98, 100, 103–4, 107, 113–14, 127–8, 142–3, 147, 149–51, 161–2, 165–6, 173–5
Hughes, Simon 18, 43, 137
Hunter, Nick 8
Hutton, Sir Leonard 88, 102
Hutton, Richard 147

Ilford 12
Illingworth, Ray 2, 77, 79, 181
Imran Khan 42
Independent Television News 97
Insole, Douglas 90, 143
Intikhab Alam 108
Inverarity, John 18–19, 137

Jackman, Robin 121, 137
Jessop, G. L. 121

Kapil Dev 18
Kent CCC 9, 141
Kent, Martin 15, 98, 104–7, 110, 117, 144, 152, 162–3, 170, 180
Knight, Roger 5
Knott, Alan 44, 53, 76, 89, 108, 123, 129, 132–3, 136, 140–2, 144, 147, 149–50, 153, 162, 166, 168, 171, 174

Lahore 40
Laird, Bruce 173
Laker, Jim 125, 161, 163
Lancashire League 79
Larkins, Wayne 53, 134, 155, 158, 165, 170
Lawry, Bill 163
Lawson, Geoff 16, 20, 22, 26–7, 29, 60, 73, 75, 79, 83, 89, 99, 137, 174
Leeds *see* Headingley

Leicester 173
Leicestershire CCC 2, 55
Lethbridge, Chris 95
Leyland, Maurice 122
Lillee, Dennis 3, 13–14, 16–17, 20–2, 26–7, 35, 46, 53, 56–8, 60–1, 64–5, 71, 75, 77, 89–90, 96, 98–101, 105–6, 108–11, 116, 127–8, 140–1, 144–7, 150, 153, 163, 165–6, 169–71, 174–5
Liverpool 120
Lloyd, Clive 86, 137
Lord's Cricket Ground 1, 7, 13, 20–1, 23, 26–7, 32, 42, 49–51, 60, 62, 79, 88, 97, 129, 132, 158, 181
Lush, Peter 96

Maidstone 44, 132
Manchester *see* Old Trafford
Mann, F. G. 38
Marsh, Rod 9, 12, 17, 22, 26, 28, 60, 64–5, 73, 75–7, 98–101, 105, 107, 110–12, 116, 140–1, 144, 146, 149, 152–4, 168, 174–5
Martin-Jenkins, Christopher 78
Marylebone CC 35, 38, 50, 88, 158; indoor cricket school 21
McFarlane, Peter 35
Medea, The 119
Melbourne 37, 74, 128, 166, 170
Middlesex CCC 1, 12, 18–19, 32, 35, 40–4, 60, 68, 85, 95, 122, 132, 158
  v Australians 9, 20–2, 46, 68
  v Essex 12, 43
  v Lancashire 81
  v Leicestershire 32
  v Nottinghamshire 44
  v Oxford University 21
  v Somerset 1, 20
  v Yorkshire 53
Miller, Geoffrey 5
Milligan, Spike 91
Multan airport 34

Muscular Dystrophy Society 56

National Westminster Cup 159
New South Wales 19, 88
New Zealand 38
'Newsnight' 7
News of the World 136
900 Days, The 119
Northampton 159
Northamptonshire CCC 155
Northern League 137
Nottingham *see* Trent Bridge
Nottinghamshire CCC 15, 53

Observer 111
Old, Chris 53, 64–5, 68–9, 71–2, 83–4, 87–90, 98, 102–4, 110, 112, 114, 133, 137, 159, 173
Oldfield, W. A. 76
Old Trafford (Manchester) 81, 113, 121, 123, 129, 142, 146, 158–9, 162, 164, 173
One-Day Internationals 18, 20, 33, 36
  England v Australia:
    Edgbaston 20
    Headingley 1, 5, 20
    Lord's 1, 5, 20
Opening Up 38
Oslear, Don 100, 103–4
Oval, Kennington 33, 39, 51, 122, 149, 151, 155, 159–62, 173–4, 180
Oxford 5
Oxford University 21

Packer, Kerry 17, 35–7, 46, 112, 167
Parker, John 161
Parker, Paul 155, 161, 164, 166, 170
Pascoe, Len 17
Perth 3, 13, 46, 61, 72, 160
Philpott, Peter 84
'Picca' *see* Dilley, Graham
Player League, John 32, 151, 159–60

Powell, Rt Hon Enoch 119
Private Eye 170
Procter, Mike 137
Prudential Trophy *see* One-Day
Internationals
Put to the Test 38

Queensland CA 17, 19, 137
'Quentin' *see* Hogg, Rodney

Rackemann, Carl 137
Radio 3 143
Radley, Clive 43
Ramsbottom CC 79
Randall, Derek 12, 109, 158
Ranjitsinhji, K. S. (Jam Saheb of Nawanagar 121
Rapley, Florence 126
Rhodes, Wilfred 122
Richards, Viv 7, 83
Roope, Graham 122
Rose, Brian 40
Roses match, The 122
'Rowdy' *see* Tavaré, Chris
Royal Wedding, The 91, 98, 102, 119, 126

St Paul's Cathedral 91
Salisbury, Harrison 119
Scarborough 41, 172
Sheffield Shield 19
Slack, Wilf 23
Smith, M. J. K. 42
Smith, Peter 96
Sobers, Sir Gary 139
Somerset CCC 1
South African Breweries Company 178
South Australia CA 22
Southend 47
Spencer, Lady Diana, Princess of Wales 91
Sporting Life 111
Sri Lanka 48, 53, 158, 175
Stenhousemuir 120
Stevenson, Graham 16

Stewart, Mickey 161
Subba Row, Raman 178
Suffolk 120
Sun 121
Sunday Express 58, 108
Sunday Times 12
Surrey CCC 39, 54, 122, 125
Swansea 111
Sydney 3, 35, 37, 49, 59, 109, 142, 161

Tate, F. W. 90
Taunton 1, 5, 41, 172
Tavaré, Chris 123, 132, 134, 138, 142, 145–7, 152, 162, 165–6, 168, 170
Taylor, Bob 23, 26, 28, 54, 70, 73, 86–8, 100, 102, 105–7, 116, 129, 133–4, 136, 174
Test and County Cricket Board 36, 57–8, 96, 178
Test Matches
Australia v England:
at Adelaide 76; at Melbourne 1, 3, 74, 166, 170, 173; at Perth 3, 13, 46, 61, 72; at Sydney 3, 59, 100, 109
Australia v India 127
v New Zealand 175; v Pakistan 175; v West Indies 175
England v Australia:
at Edgbaston 46, 91, 94–117, 120–7, 129, 132, 146–7, 152, 173–4, 180; at Headingley 48, 50–90, 97, 113, 117, 119–20, 126, 132, 143, 172, 180; at Lord's 23, 26–32, 49–51, 60, 88, 95, 129, 181; at Old Trafford 108, 112–13, 123, 129, 138–54, 158–9, 165, 173; at The Oval 62, 151, 155, 158–71, 180; at Trent Bridge 7, 9–29, 59–62, 88
England v India 3, 5, 129, 149, 180
v Pakistan 91; v West Indies 1, 15, 20, 134, 173

Thomas, Bernard 8, 52, 62, 87, 91, 107, 109

Thomson, Jeff 3, 17–19, 21–3, 31, 35, 44, 60, 64, 137

Times, The 34

Titmus, Fred 111

Todd, Ian 121

Trent Bridge (Nottingham) 8–9, 12–16, 47, 59–61, 78, 88, 180

Trueman, Fred 143

Tyson, Frank 88

Underwood, Derek 3, 53, 94, 108, 113, 123, 125, 129, 132, 136, 139, 159–60

United Nations Black List 139, 177

Uxbridge 41

van der Bijl, Vintcent 17, 41

Victoria CA 60

Wadsworth, Ken 168

Wales, Prince and Princess of 91

Walker, Max 19

Warwickshire CCC 52, 54, 95

Welham, Dirk 161, 167–8

West Bengal CA 159

Western Australia CA 13, 17, 173

Westminster School Foundation Dinner 119

Whitney 19, 137, 140, 142, 147, 149, 154, 164–5, 170

Willey, Peter 13, 26–7, 53, 55, 57, 61, 63, 65, 70, 72, 75, 79–80, 83, 85, 87, 100–1, 109, 134, 136

Willis, Bob 4, 13, 28, 39, 46, 48, 51–2, 57, 59, 61–2, 64, 68–73, 79, 84, 86–90, 94 8, 102–6, 111–14, 125, 127, 133, 138, 140, 143–4, 153–4, 160–4, 166–8, 173

Wilson, Don 50

Wood, Graeme 21, 28–9, 59, 69, 75, 86, 100–3, 107, 112, 140, 143, 150, 162, 166–7

Woodcock, John 34, 71

'Wooden Top' *see* Botham, Ian

Woolmer, Bob 9, 13, 26, 28, 50, 85, 134, 140, 159

Worcester 41

World Series Cricket 35–7, 112, 178

Yallop, Graham 13, 15, 22, 60, 72, 79, 86, 88, 103, 105, 114, 116, 112–3, 150–2, 162–3, 166, 168, 173–4

Yorkshire 33, 51, 62, 70, 111, 132, 158, 160

Yorkshire Post 34

'Zap' *see* Gooch, Graham